LAKE WINDERMERE, GRASMERE & CONISTON WATER

THROUGH TIME

Gill Jepson

AMBERLEY

This book is dedicated to my Lake District ancestors and family

First published 2018

Amberley Publishing
The Hill, Stroud, Gloucestershire, GL5 4EP
www.amberley-books.com

ISBN 978 1 4456 8193 1 (print)
ISBN 978 1 4456 8194 8 (ebook)

British Library Cataloguing in Publication Data.
A catalogue record for this book is available from the British Library.

Origination by Amberley Publishing.
Printed in Great Britain.

Introduction

Living in the Furness area I am very familiar with the South Lakes and have personal and familial connections there. The region is so much more than the chocolate-box pictures we are used to seeing. It has its own distinctive history and each of the three areas, although interlinked, are still unique entities. I have taken the liberty of claiming three lesser-known lakes as part of this book's mandate as well as the three named. I have done this because they are so close geographically, and they have impacted upon the environment and visitor focus of the area.

The book encompasses a vast area, including villages, lakes, rivers and strange stories and interesting people. The natural beauty of the Lake District has long been a magnet for artists, writers and crafts people of all kinds, and this tradition continues. Each personality has left their own mark and legacy one way or another, some effecting change to the environment and nature of the place, others glorifying it for posterity through their own creativity. The ordinary people who live and work here are witnesses to these changes and viewpoints and are the often-forgotten cogs in the wheel of tourism which is one of the largest employers in the area.

The Lake District is a strange paradox in some ways; it tries hard to retain its authenticity and true nature, yet this is threatened by the lifeblood of the area – tourism. One can't help but lament the modern cultural changes creeping in, such as the well-known 'chains' of cafés and shops in places like Bowness. The very uniqueness of the 'Lakeland' experience is being pushed out by boutique hotels, high street chains, and eating places of all types and origins jockeying for position with the more traditional tea shops, pubs and quaint shops. It isn't that the Lakes should be preserved in aspic exactly, but it is sad to see its villages starting to look like everywhere else. Wordsworth, Ruskin, Potter and Rawnsley would be hard-pressed to find their world as they left it despite the ideals which fed into the National Trust intending to conserve the Lakeland way of life.

As in many such places the Lakes is faced with the problem of seasonal work, low wages, limited housing and difficult transport links. The beauty and the heritage are still in evidence, but more and more young people are leaving the area to find work and affordable housing, being outpriced by 'offcomers' with more disposable income and second homes. Add to this the constant drive of commercialism, not to mention the new status as a World Heritage Site, which will surely bring in even more visitors and the attendant problems, which though securing the prosperity of the area, might damage it too.

The research for the book was enjoyable and revealing and I have included the stories of the famous and the ordinary people linked to the Lakes. Sometimes accessing the views and locations depicted was quite difficult. Finding such places as Poet's Seat was trial and error – located on a very busy road with no parking, it meant many visits had to be undertaken. Some places were particularly shocking as the location had almost disappeared. However, the experience was refreshing and re-engaged me with a much-loved place, one that Cumbrians like me are delighted to share. The pictures were mostly taken in the off-peak season to better capture the essence of the Lake District. However, had these been taken in summer many of the views would be obscured by a myriad of tourists and visitors. I felt very privileged to have the time to 'wander' in the footsteps of the likes of Wordsworth, Ruskin and Potter and enjoy the same uplifting scenery that they enjoyed, though I do wonder about their fitness as opposed to mine – some of the hills they surmounted at a great age were quite a challenge.

Essentially, those things which attracted the early visitors to the Lakes are still the same. You can still find tranquillity and peace if you look hard enough, and in any weather or season the views are still spectacular. I hope I have captured the essence of the district, but as with any book like this it can never be complete or definitive. I am sure I have enough material for another book and it is impossible to include every beauty spot or favourite location, but I hope I have included the important ones.

Gill Jepson, 2018

Newby Bridge

The attractive stone bridge with five arches, dating from 1651, has always been a significant crossing. It crosses the River Leven and is at the head of Lake Windermere. It is a crucial junction connecting with the route along Windermere to Hawkshead. It is greatly congested these days, succumbing to cars, coaches and heavy traffic. The distinctive triangular gaps are now essential for any one on foot walking across, providing a refuge against the oncoming traffic. The tranquillity has gone forever and even in the off season it remains busy. The quiet hamlet is overlooked by the A590, the only main road in and out of the Furness peninsula and the delays on the bridge arise from the difficulty in exiting onto the road. This picture is one of a set of postcards produced by Raphael Tuck, for Furness Railway, based in Barrow-in-Furness. Each one had the Furness Railway stamp and declared proudly that the railway passed through 'the Lake District and some of the most beautiful coastal scenery in the Kingdom'. Each has the name of the railway station in which it was sold, and which was closest to the scene depicted. The company were quick to recognise the potential of the tourist industry and capitalise upon it.

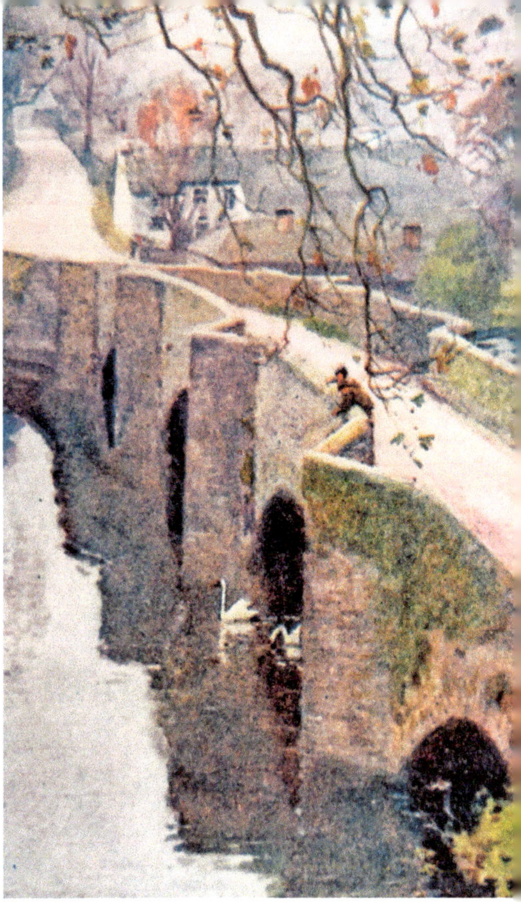

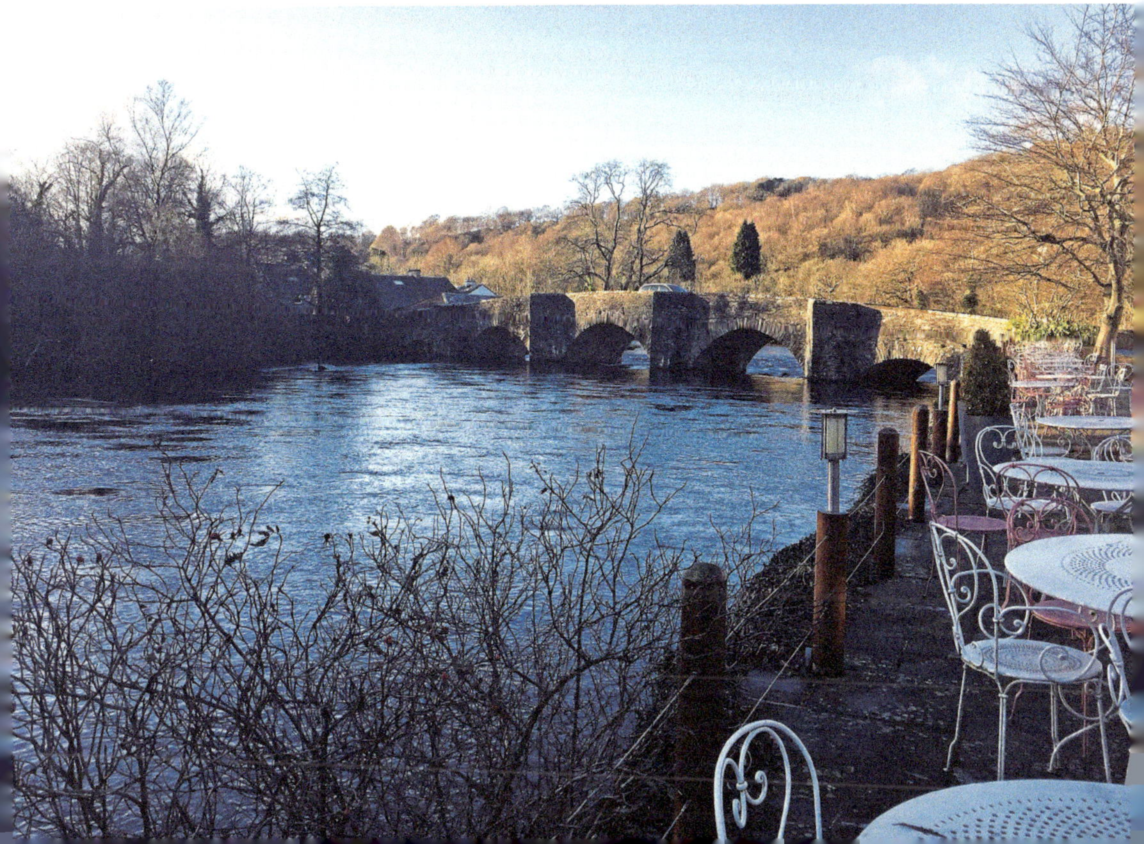

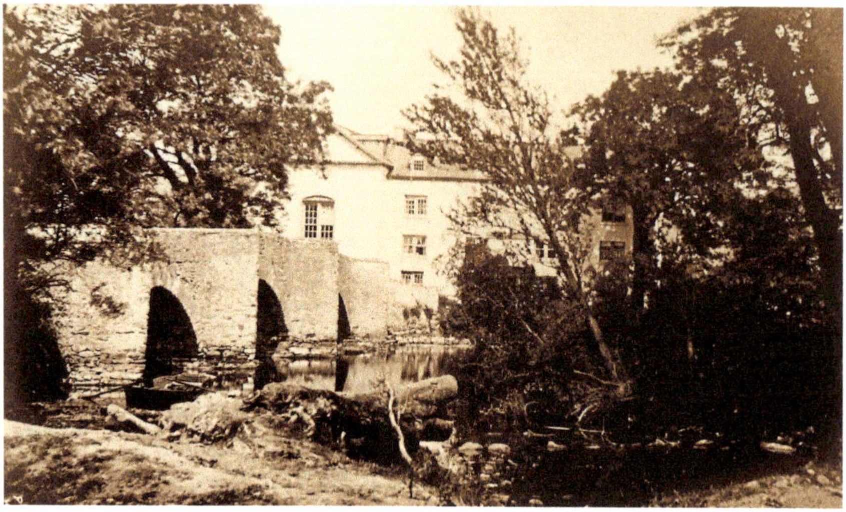

The Swan at Newby Bridge

This inn was an important staging post and in the nineteenth century it became a key place for the tourist industry. There are several other inns and hotels in the close vicinity of the Swan Hotel, which retains many of its older features. It has been extended over the years and is a popular spa hotel these days. Unfortunately, it has struggled with flooding in recent years and remains vulnerable to rising levels of both the river and the lake. Across the busy A590 is another hotel, the Newby Bridge Hotel. The Newby Bridge Mansion, as it was called, was built by James Machel in 1793, who held a lineage leading back to the twelfth-century Lord Ulf. This was one of the earliest large mansions to be built on the edge of Windermere. Apparently, William Wordsworth was a family friend who stayed there often. The house is now a hotel and displays one of Wordsworth's poems; he later objected to the continued building of villas and houses, believing them to be a blight on his beloved lakes, but presumably he approved of this one. Arthur Ransome, the writer of *Swallows and Amazons*, was a regular visitor too and he probably exploited the sailing opportunities available on the lake during his stay, of which he so often wrote.

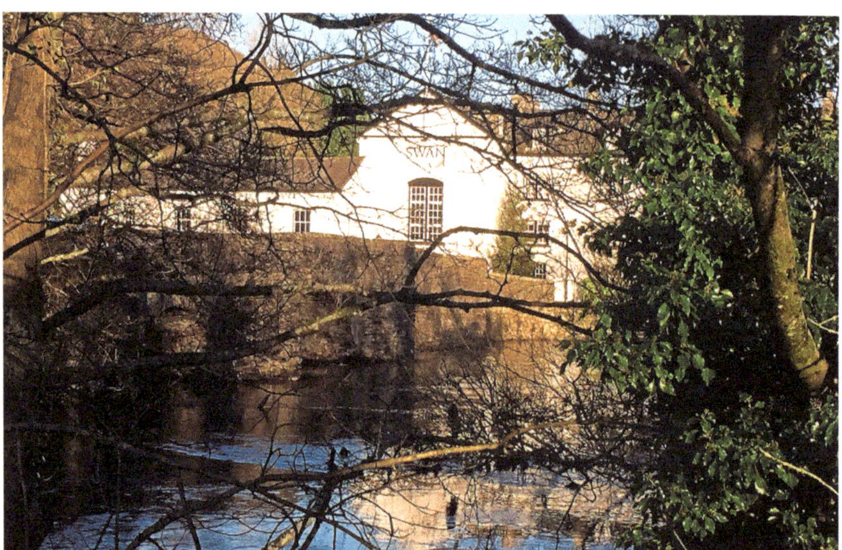

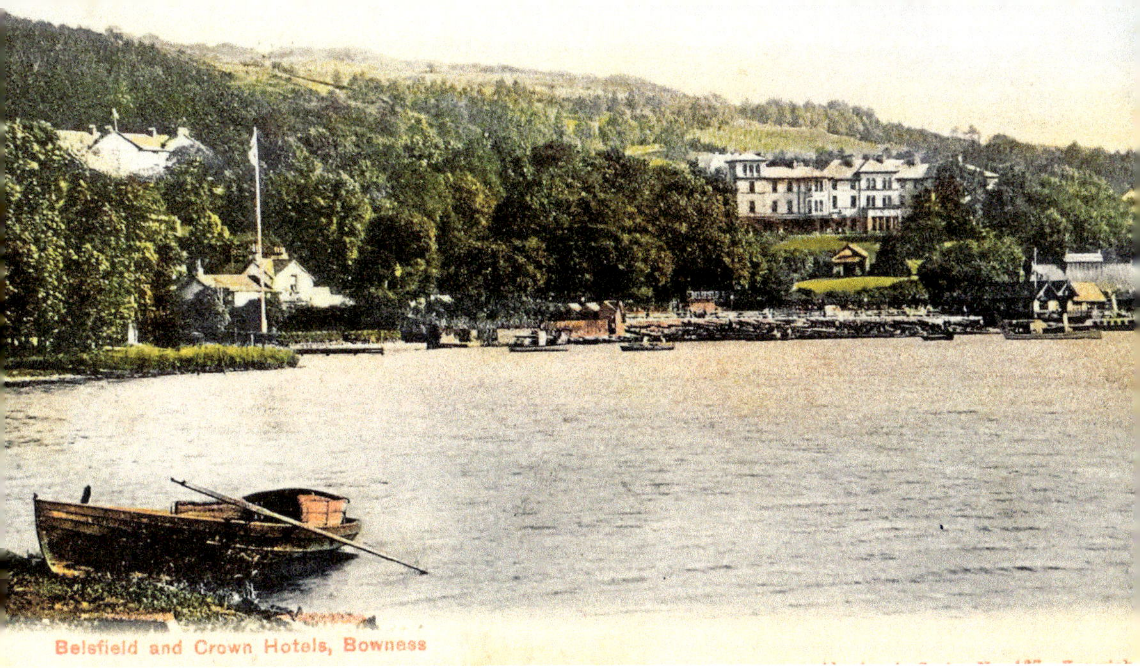

View across Windermere to the Belsfield Hotel

Looking across the lake the Belsfield Hotel is easily visible and still dominates the view. The Victorian Gothic boat sheds and ticket booths are still resplendent and in use. The visitor numbers are significantly higher than when these buildings were constructed, and the shoreline is littered with modern street furniture such as signage, traffic lights and crossings. Although one can still take out a simple rowing boat from the piers, the predominant water vessels are the larger pleasure boats. The contemporary photograph presents a quiet appearance, but this belies the bay's popularity in the height of the summer season. Traffic clogs the main road through the village and tourists mill about the beach, feeding the swans and ducks, eating chips and ice cream and participating in that very British occupation of queuing. The overall impression is far from the sedate tourism of the nineteenth century and is more reminiscent of any popular seaside resort.

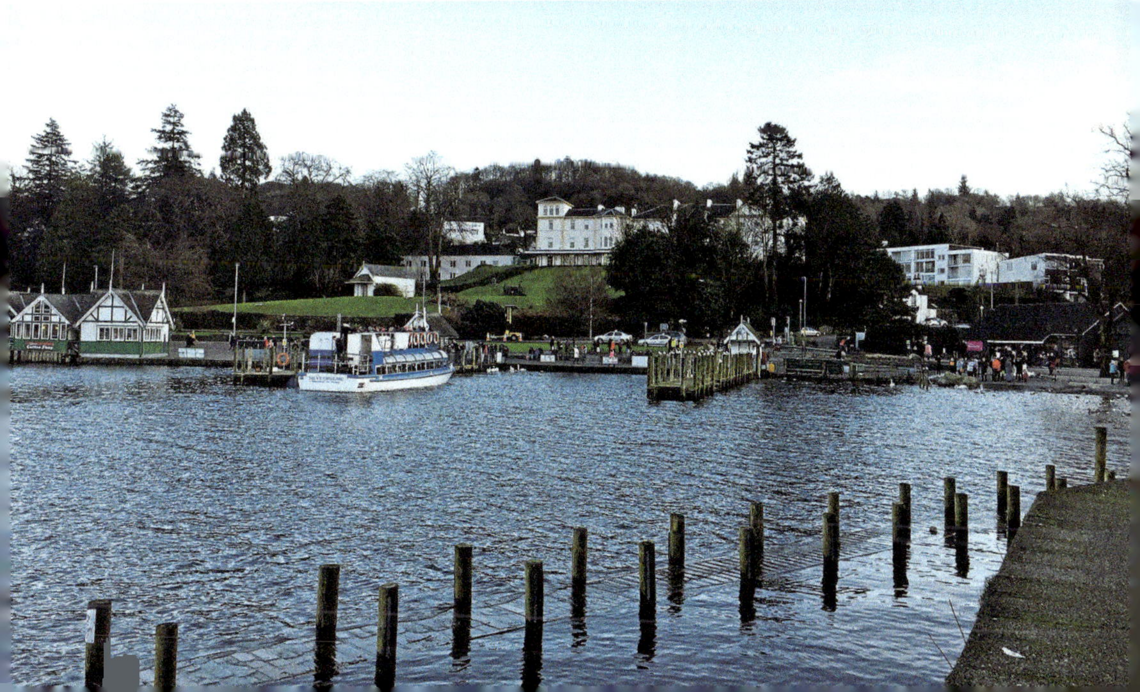

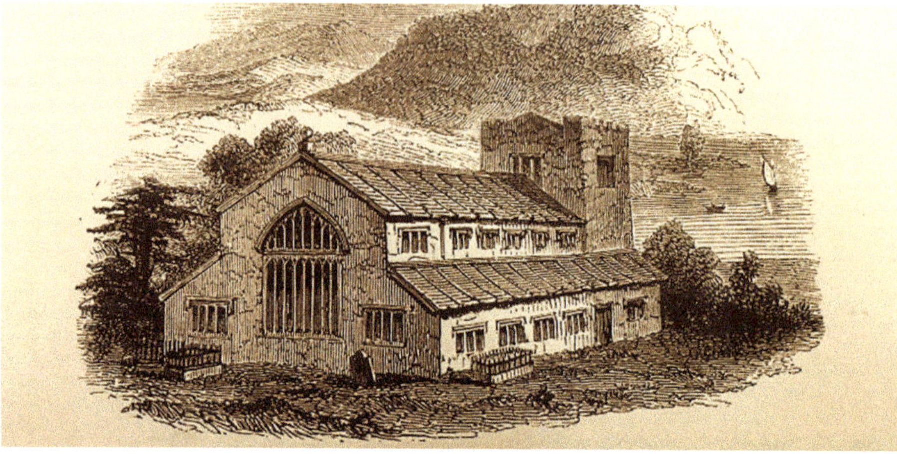

St Martin's Church, Bowness

This twelfth-century church was destroyed by fire in 1480, the only remnant left being the font and the base of the tower. St Martin's was later restored in 1870 by Paley and Austin who extended the chancel and raised the tower to its current height, adding a saddleback roof and replacing the seating. The changes are distinct when comparing the engraving from 1840 to the modern photograph. H W Schneider, the local iron magnate, was one of the benefactors who paid for the building work. Ancient inscriptions and paintings were discovered beneath the plaster, indicating its medieval origins. Henry Hughes of London painted elaborate murals and restored the glass in the East Window, but carefully conserving some medieval glass, possibly from Cartmel Priory. Other minor changes were made in the intervening years to provide suitable accommodation for a modern congregation. On one of the arches there is a thanksgiving poem dated 1629, following the Gunpowder Plot; some ancient books are on display; and the coat of arms of George Washington's grandfather can be seen. Outside one can find the grave of a freed slave called Rasselas Belfield (d. 1822), possibly the valet of Peter Taylor of Belsfield House. Ironically, against the west wall is a slab to John Bolton, slave trader and plantation owner, who died in 1837.

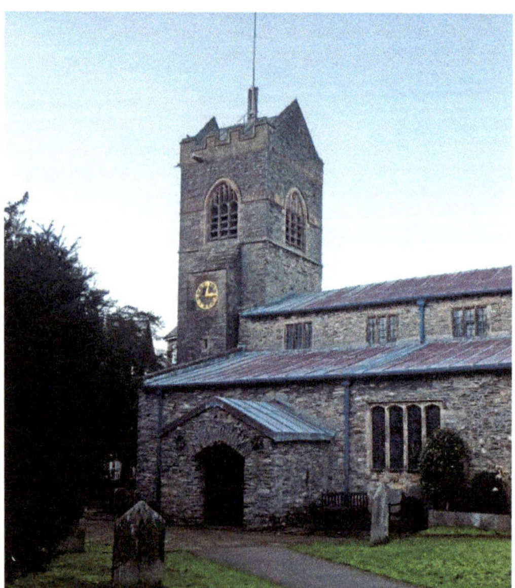

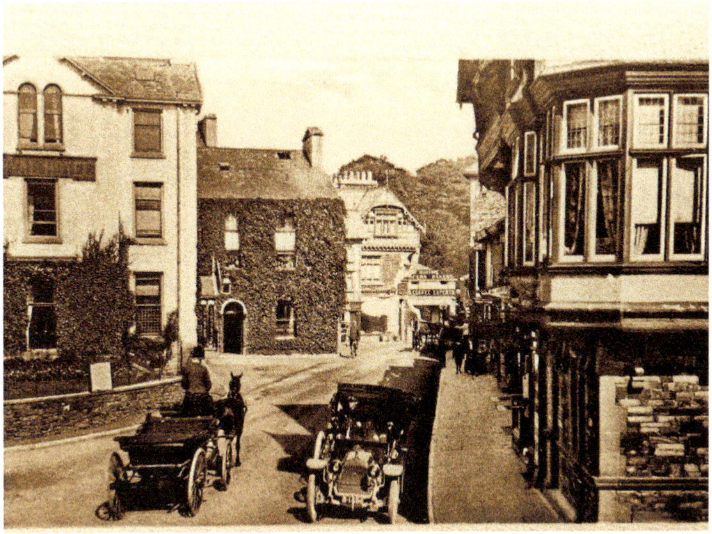

The Royal Hotel, Bowness

The view along the street towards the Royal Hotel in Bowness on first examination does not appear to have altered greatly. However, when compared, the two photographs reveal some interesting changes. The Royal Hotel is no longer there in its original form; it has been adapted and modernised to accommodate a glass conservatory, which completely alters the nature of the building. The modern outlet is a Costa Coffee shop, providing refreshments more akin to city life than a Lakeland village. Its incongruity is probably only lessened when you realise that there is a Tesco store further along. The building in the middle appears to be different or altered but the main view looks the same. The trees at the rear of the earlier picture have gone, replaced by other buildings and the road is more congested in the modern photo. The volume of traffic and tourists is huge during the summer months and even in winter, when this photo was taken it is much busier than in earlier times. The rurality of Bowness is very much compromised these days and with the addition of more retail outlets, bistros, curry houses and the like, the essence of the Lakeland experience is far removed from that which the early tourists sought.

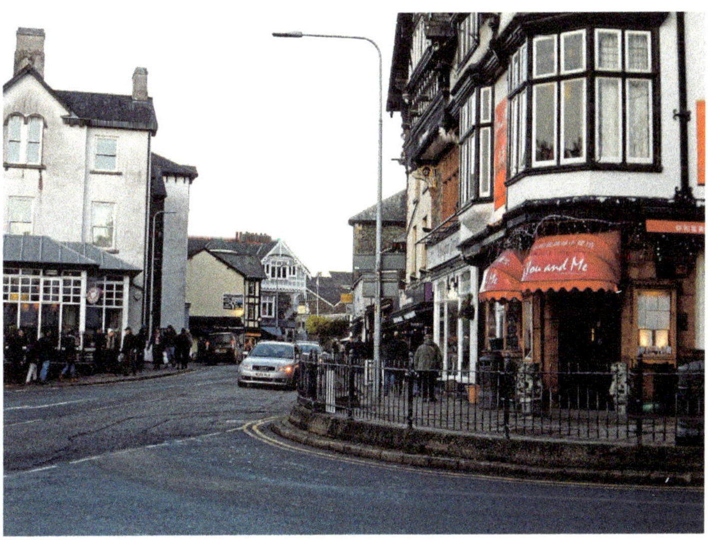

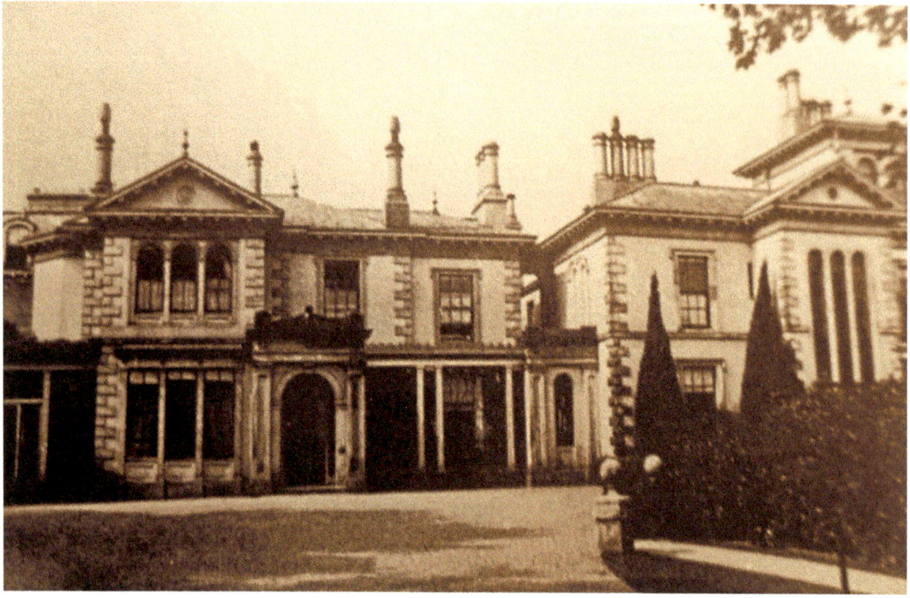

The Belsfield Hotel, Windermere

Nowadays yet another boutique hotel, Belsfield began life as private mansion built for the Baroness von Sternberg in 1845. In 1869 the industrialist Henry W. Schneider made the house his country residence. He built a private pier on the lakeside so that he could indulge his love of sailing and to maintain his prominence as a Victorian gentleman. His steam yacht *The Esperance* was moored at the pier and Schneider breakfasted on the boat each day, sailing down the lake to the station to take the train to Barrow-in-Furness. He read his post on the journey and was swiftly transported to Barrow by train from Lakeside to begin the business of the day. *The Esperance* was the inspiration for Uncle Jim's boat in *Swallows and Amazons* written by Arthur Ransome. Schneider had other homes, but Belsfield was his main one and he died there at the age of seventy-two on 11 November 1887. He was buried in Bowness cemetery, in view of the lake and the home he loved.

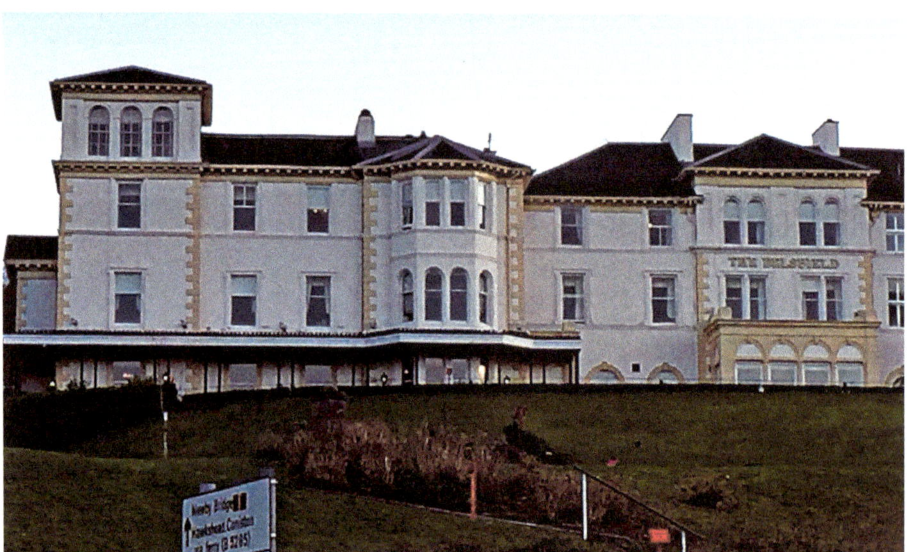

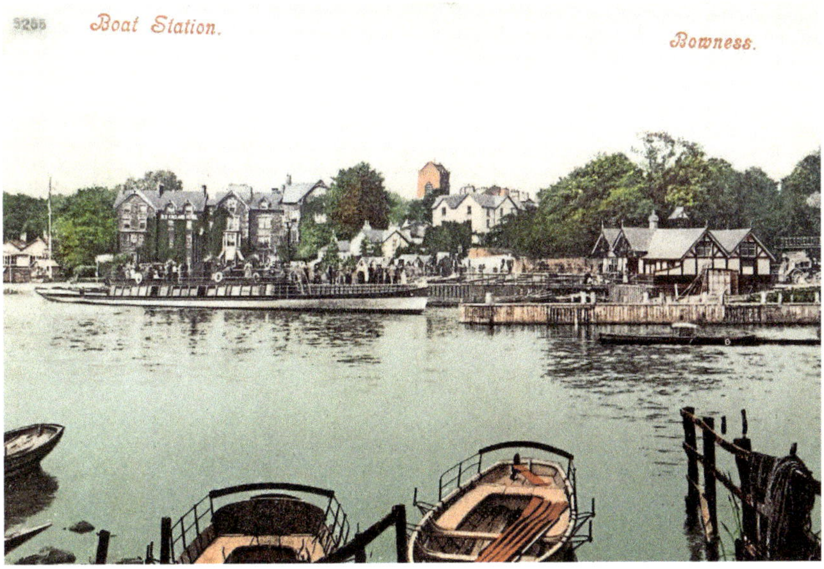

Bowness and the Old England Hotel

Looking across Lake Windermere towards the Old England Hotel one can see that the vista is structurally unchanged. Many of the buildings in view are within the conservation area, so they are mostly retained in their original form. The conservation area designation demonstrates the importance of the village historically. It was originally a Norse trading post and settlement which developed into a small town in the medieval period. Its growth continued, and grand villas and houses were built along the shore of the lake by nineteenth-century industrialists and businessmen – 'offcomers' as they were known locally. The Old England is a Grade II-listed building and began life as a private residence. It was turned into a hotel in the late nineteenth century in the same way as the Belfield, in response to the popularity of the lakes and the influx of visitors. The piers and jetties remain the same and the Victorian Gothic ticket booths have been preserved, maintaining the nineteenth-century flavour at the lake edge.

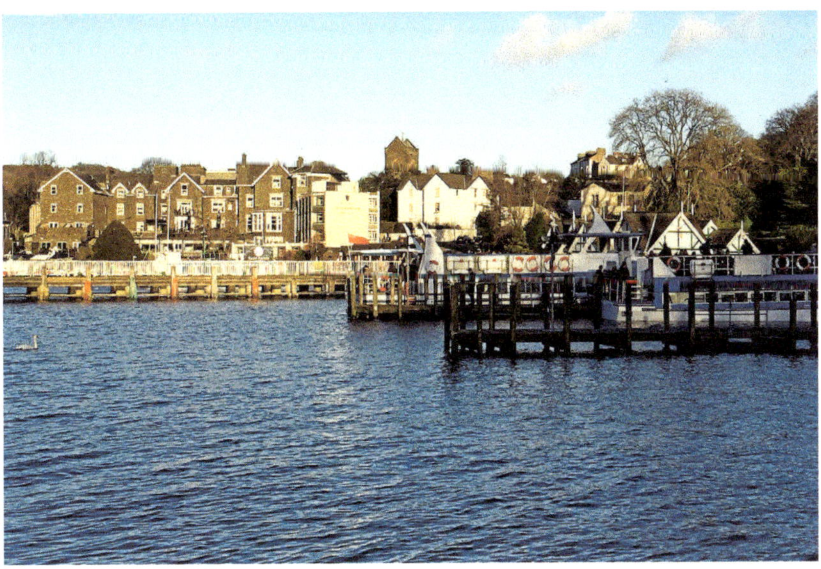

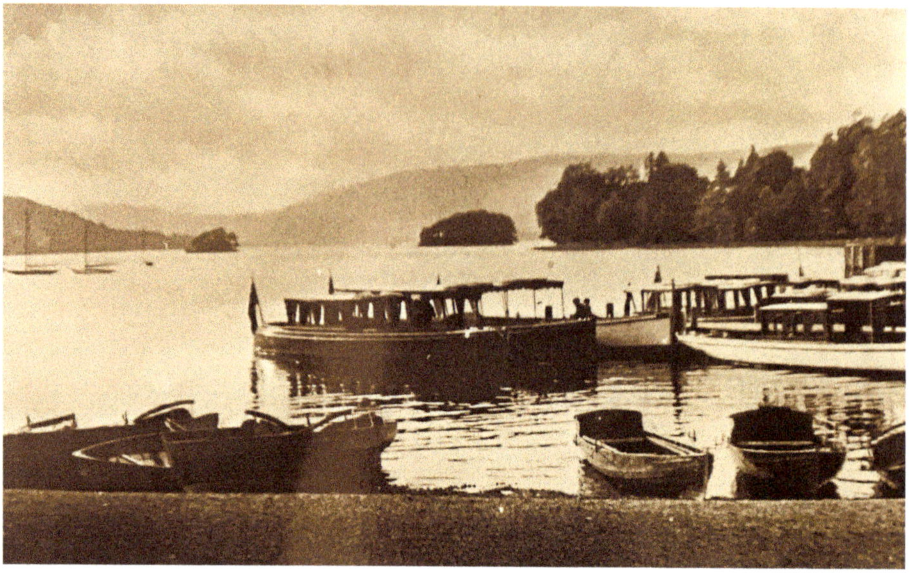

Bowness Bay, Windermere

The building of villas was abhorred by William Wordsworth, who challenged these as being out of character with the natural countryside. He was concerned about an influx of tourists and commented that the lakes as entertainment should be confined to those who truly appreciated it, so that 'they could be safe from the molestation of cheap trains pouring out their hundreds at a time along the margin of Windermere'. He had come into conflict with Furness Railway before over the building of the line close to Furness Abbey at Barrow-in-Furness. He can probably claim to be the world's first 'nimby' (not in my back yard), but when one looks at the most popular Lakeland destinations today, one can see what he was getting at. It appears to be a necessary oxymoron that the Lake District needs tourism to survive, yet the volume of tourists is slowly destroying the nature of the place. It would be very interesting to see what Mr Wordsworth would make of the Lakes now with its 'boutique' hotels, curry houses, fish and chip shops and potential zip wires.

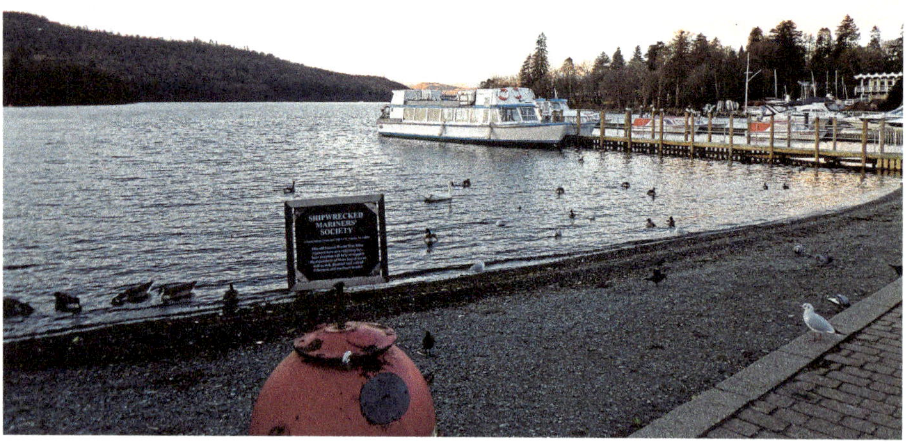

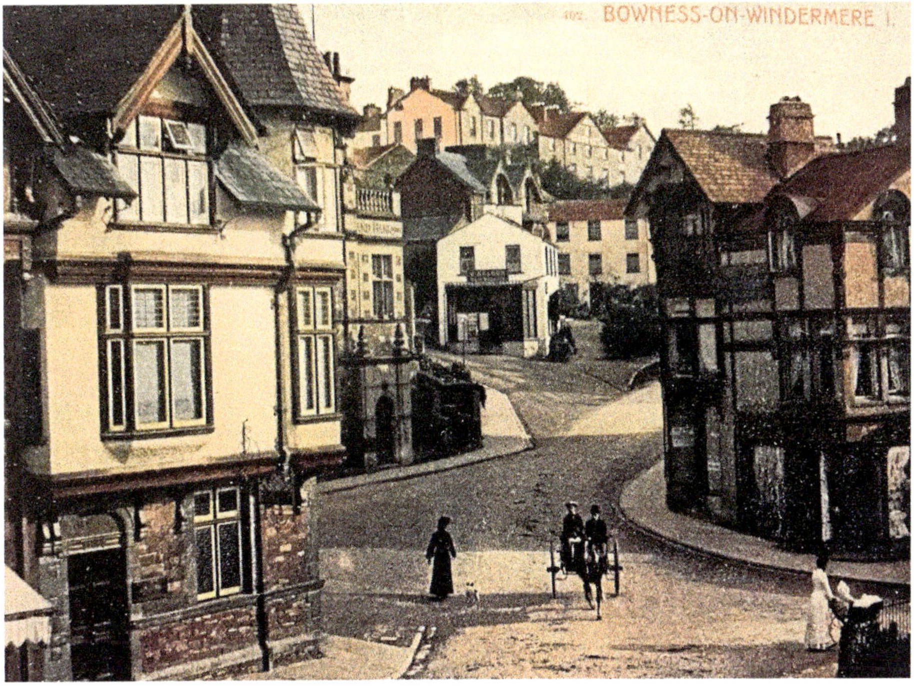

Bowness Village

The charming picture of the village captures the flavour of the Victorian Lakeland village. The traffic comprises of one pony and trap and a mere handful of pedestrians. Once again, the greatest difference noticed is the level of traffic. The village is very busy now and cars are constantly driving through. The older picture provides us with what seems to be a calmer, quieter time and the street is clear of street furniture and signage. The shops and buildings appear to be small businesses, there to serve the community rather than the many tourists that would later descend on Bowness.

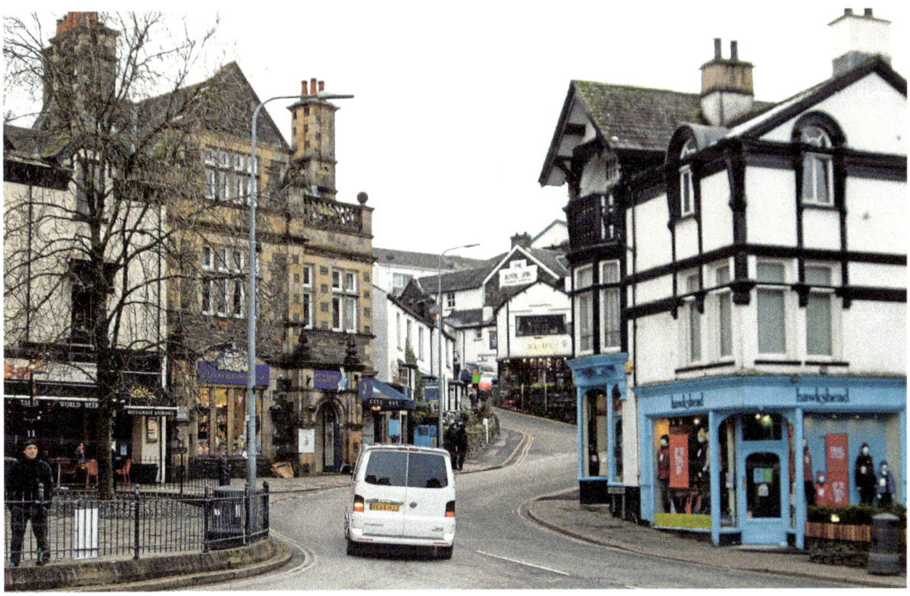

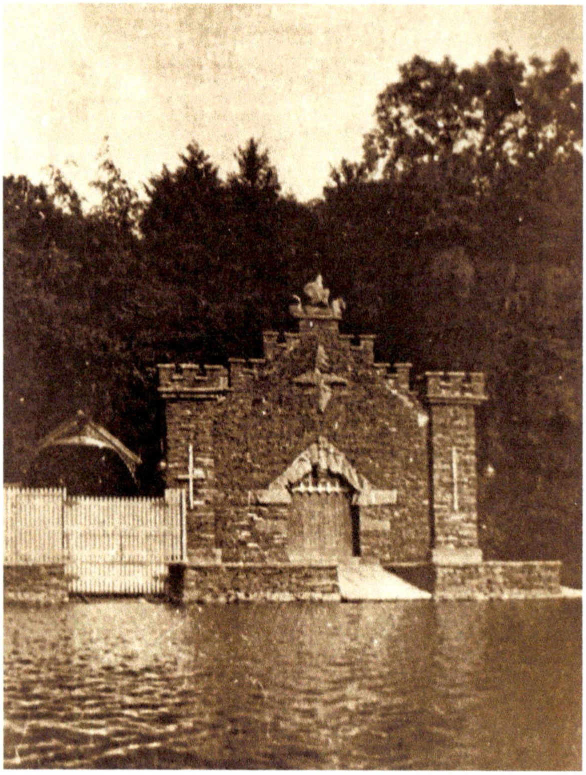

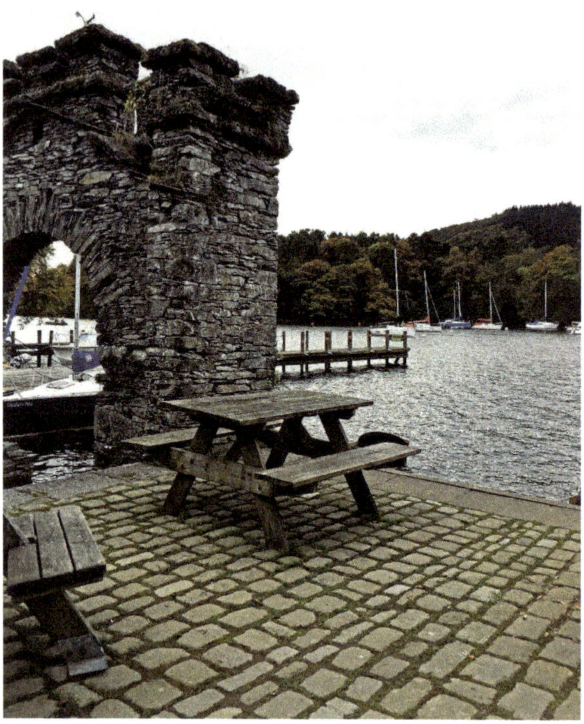

Fell Foot

This country park has had many incarnations over time and it began as the fording point across the lake from Kendal into Furness, governed by the monks at Furness Abbey. It later became a farm belonging to the Robinsons, a family of yeoman farmers. It was sold in 1784 to a Leeds merchant, Jeremiah Dixon, who built yet another impressive villa on the shores of the lake. The road had been pushed further inland around 1810, creating a small estate. In 1813 the property was sold to Francis Dukinfield Astley of Manchester, another aspiring 'gentleman' industrialist who made his fortune from coal mining. Squire Astley, as he was known, was a keen huntsman and was interested in forestry too, which is evident from the landscaping of the grounds. His son sold the property in 1859 to Col George John Miller Ridehalgh, Lord of Urmston Manor in Manchester. Ridehalgh carried on the sporting tradition of being a huntsman and keen sailor and it is he we must thank for the Gothic boathouses and piers that we see today. The final owner demolished Ridehalgh's beloved house in 1907 to create an even grander one. The plans were abandoned when he died, and the estate later passed to the National Trust in 1948. (Photo courtesy of National Trust)

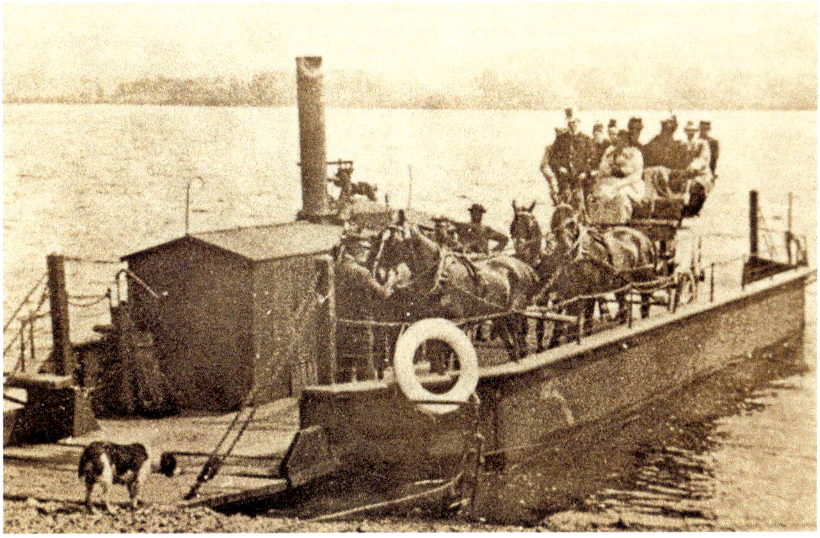

Ferry Nab, Windermere

There has been a ferry crossing on Windermere for over 500 years, initially to enable the monks of Furness Abbey to traverse the lake. The long length of the lake demanded crossings to provide direct access to the various settlements. Originally, the ferry was a simple rowing boat. Later, as technology progressed, this gave way to steam power and then diesel. The position of the ferry is around the midpoint of the lake and connects Far Sawrey to Bowness. The current cable ferry runs daily throughout the year and shortens the journey by 15 miles. The ferrymen are recorded in the story of the Claife Crier, who was a lovelorn monk from Furness Abbey who had been rejected by a lady of dubious morals from Claife Heights. He took rejection badly and died crying for his lost love. His cries continued through time. Ferrymen ignored these until one foolhardy soul crossed to pick up the fare. The ferryman returned the next morning, incoherent with fear and dying shortly after. A monk from Lady Holme chantry exorcised the ghost and committed him to cry in the quarry 'until men can walk dry-shod across the lake'.

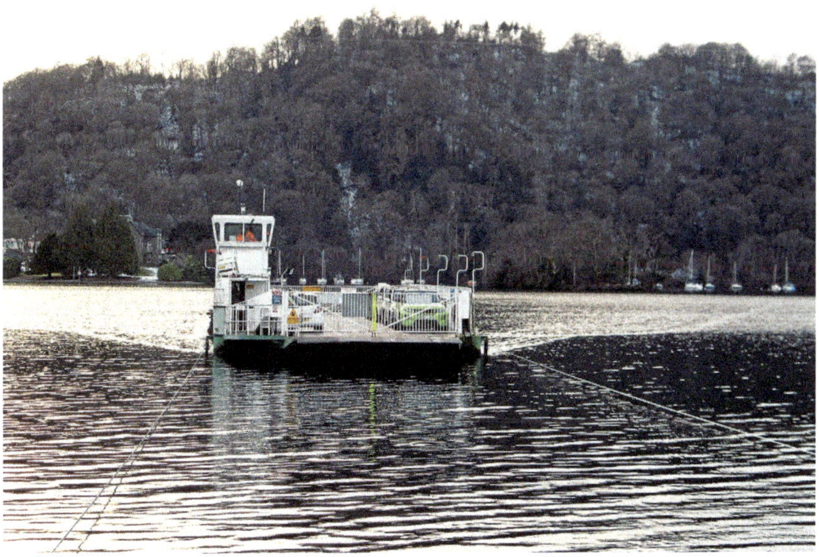

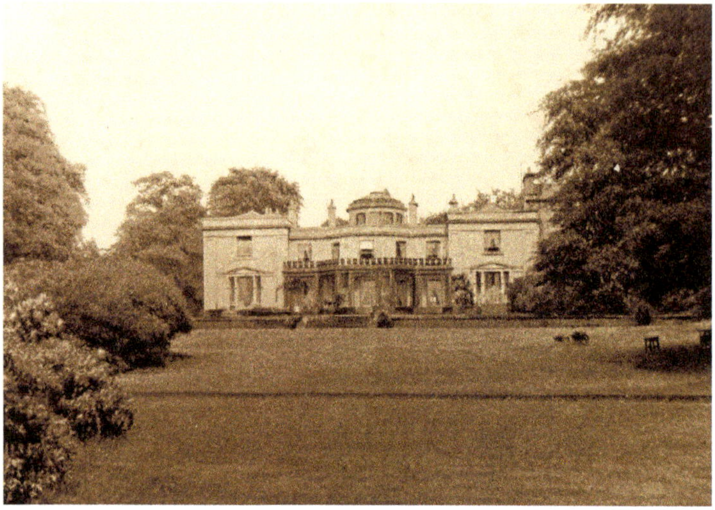

Storrs Hall, Windermere

A dark history hides behind the beauty of this mansion. It was built in the late 1790s for Sir John Legard, 6th Baronet of Ganton in Yorkshire; it was he who built the Temple of Heroes, celebrating British Naval victories, in the grounds. The house was sold in 1804 to David Pike Watts, a London wine merchant and uncle of the famous painter John Constable. Constable stayed at Storrs in 1806 during his tour of the Lake District. The house was extensively remodelled by John Gandy at this time. The next owner, John Bolton was a colourful character who came from humble beginnings in Ulverston. He worked for Rawlinson and Chorley, West India merchants, and once he had accrued enough money he set up his own business in 1786. He became successful and rich, principally from the slave trade. He was influential in Liverpool, politically and commercially, but his notoriety grew when he killed Major Brooks in a duel in 1805. His country life was devoted to social events and regattas. He had many illustrious friendships with the likes of Wordsworth and Professor John Wilson and he entertained Canning, Sir Walter Scott and Robert Southey. After Bolton died the house was sold and became a hotel in 1892 under Benjamin Townson of Barrow. It recently underwent renovation by the current owner and is a popular venue for weddings.

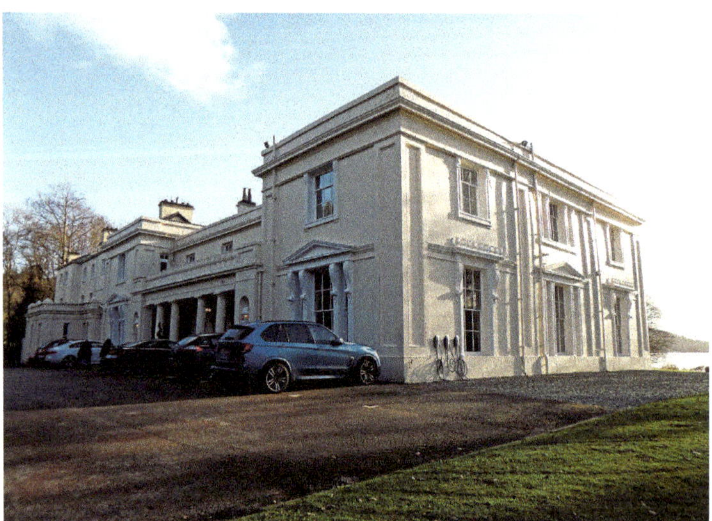

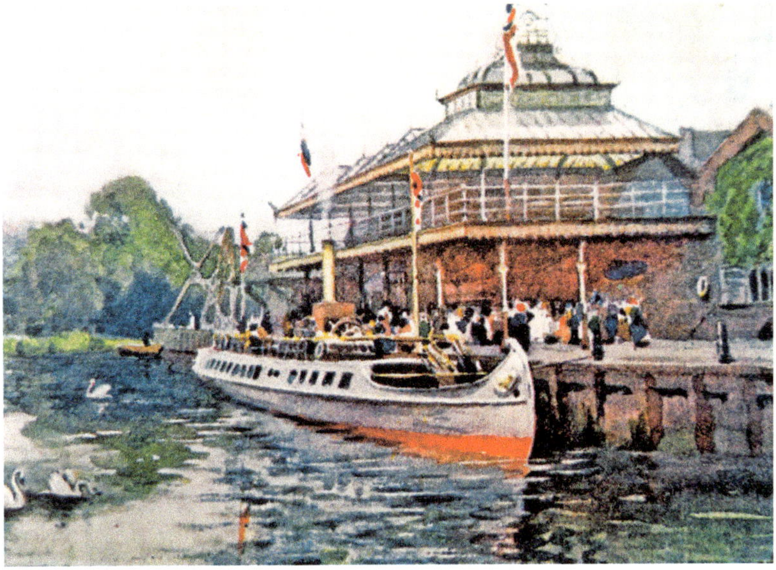

Refreshment Pavilion, Lakeside

It is not difficult to imagine Lakeside in its Victorian heyday. The views remain the same and hints of the Gothic buildings are visible. There are moorings in both pictures and the 'steamers' still begin their trips from here. The new car park intrudes significantly into the scene and the lovely glass roof of the pavilion has been removed in favour of a much less aesthetically pleasing upper floor. The current tearoom is a modern functional space with little Victorian charm left; those wanting a more authentic experience should seek it in the more traditional hotel. Some of the ironwork remains and the alterations have not completely obliterated the original building. The changes reflect the demands of modern tourists for quick turnover and fast food. Naturally, to welcome visitors who arrive by car a good deal of the site has been taken up by the necessary evil of the car park and during peak season the area is inundated with visitors.

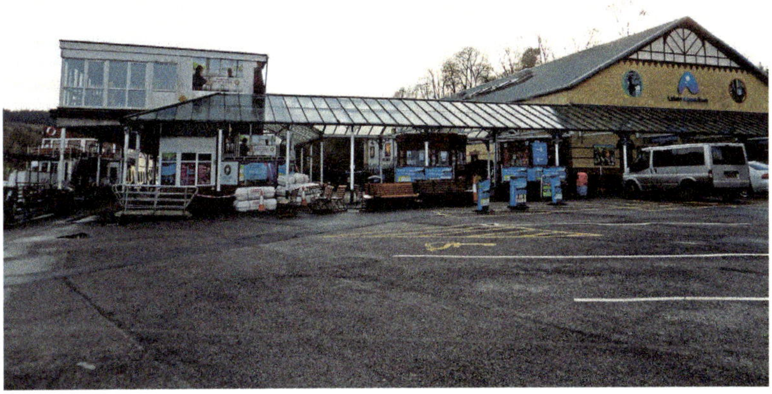

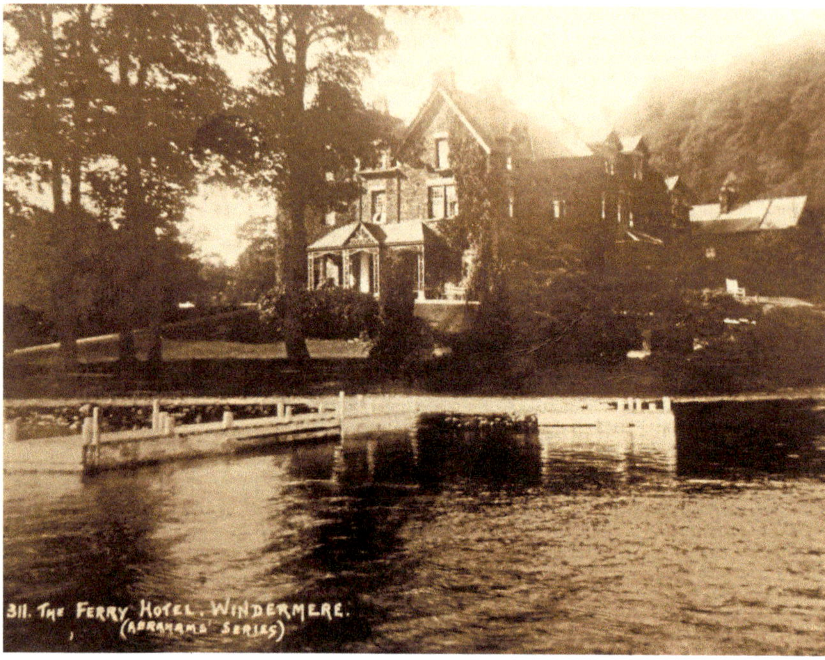

The Ferry Hotel, Windermere

At first glance this hotel has hardly changed over time. The view of it from the lake is slightly obscured by trees, but it is still identifiable. The position is ideal, overlooking the lake and ferry, from which it takes its name. The Ferry Hotel replaced an earlier hostelry called the Ferry Inn in 1881. A girls' school was relocated here for safety in the Second World War. Later the Freshwater Biological Association acquired the building for a time in 1948. The hotel has been extended over the years and of course gardens have given way to a car park.

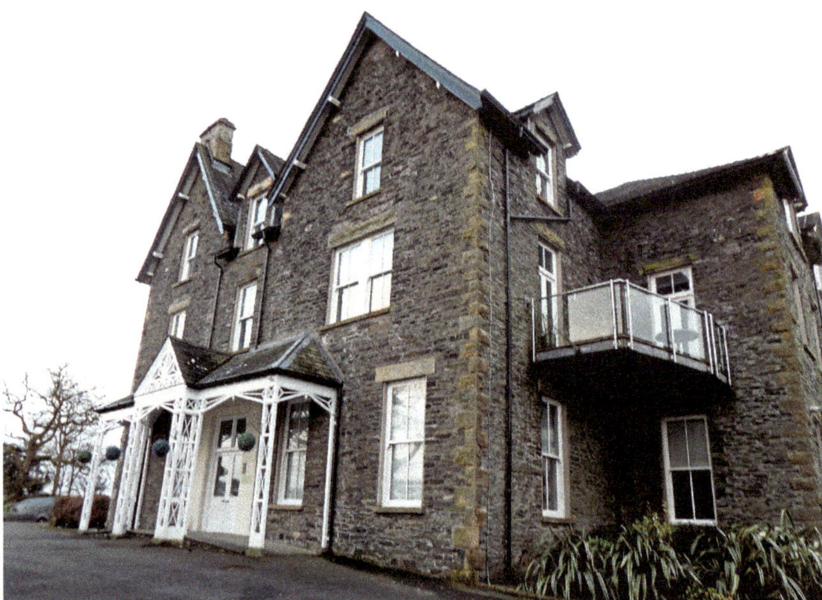

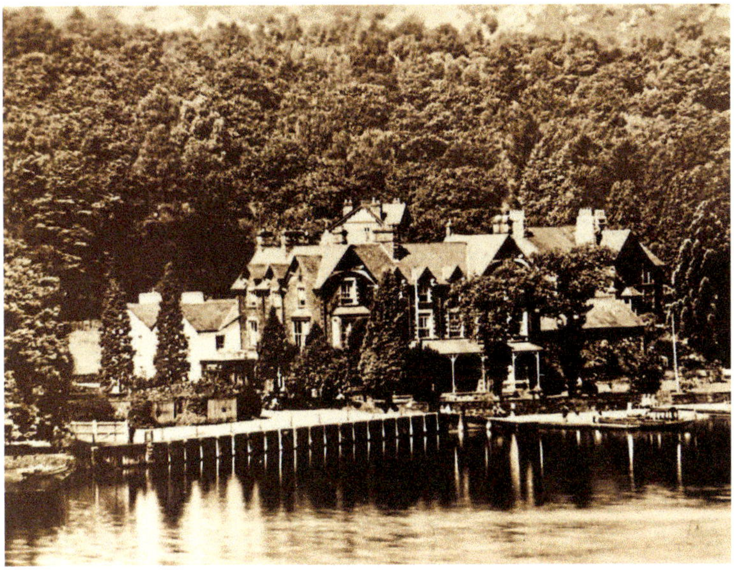

Lakeside Hotel

This began life as a seventeenth-century coaching inn. It was a staging post connecting the industrial areas of Lancashire and Yorkshire, bringing workers to the various mills and industry in the Newby Bridge area. It was a hub for transport links, including the Lakeside and Haverthwaite Railway and the Windermere Steamers. This brought the hotel more business and expansion. The hotel now is much larger than the one in the early picture. The building has been extended in keeping with the Gothic style and the addition of the Victorian-style conservatories enhance the hotel and amplifies the historic nature of it. The foreshore has been developed into gardens where guests can sit at tables and there are jetties for small boats. The entrance is maintained in the same manner, but the car parking facilities detract from the overall look of the place. It is a popular venue for weddings and celebrations and afternoon teas overlooking the lake.

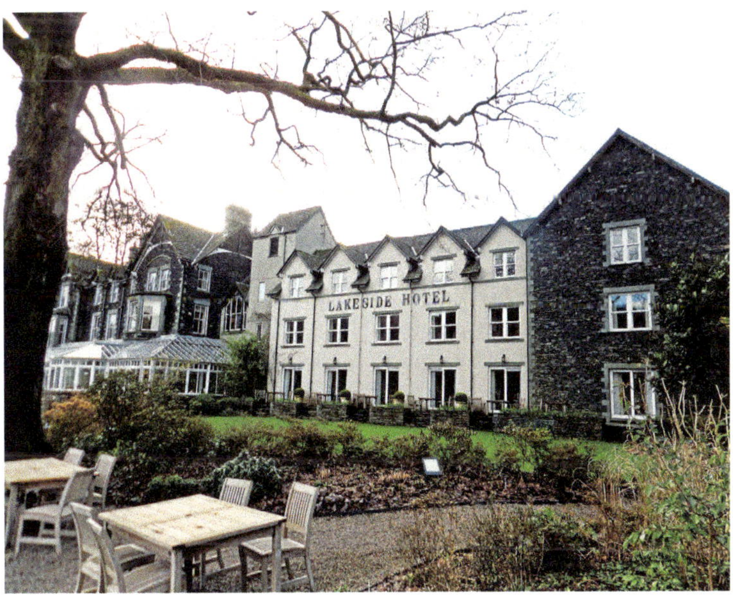

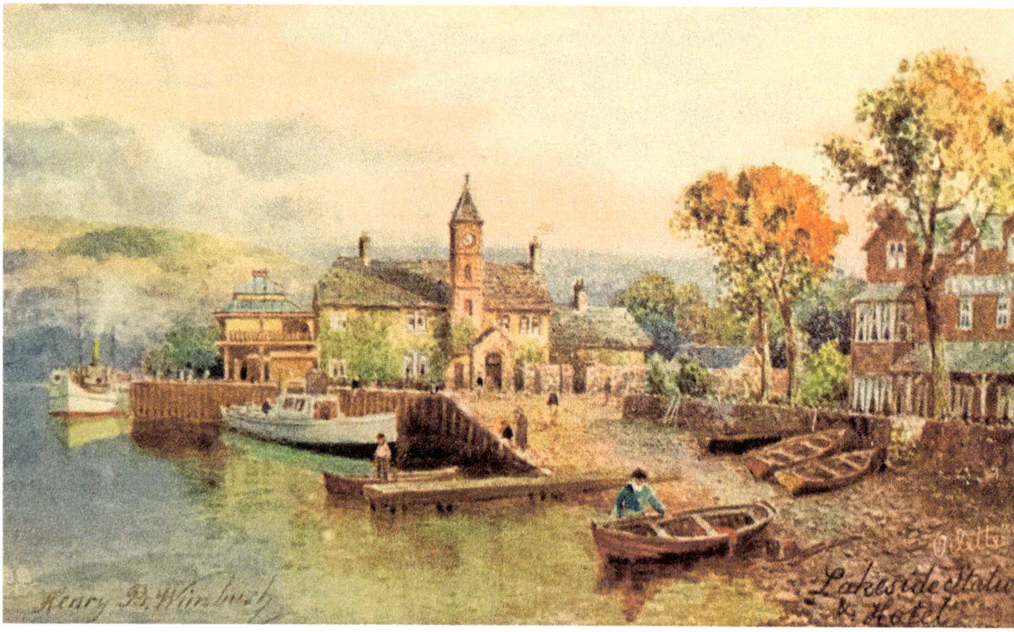

Lakeside Hotel and Station

The Lakeside Hotel has extended in size and takes up more of the site than before, but this has been done sympathetically. The difference is apparent in the two photographs, the shore line in the earlier one being less formal and easily accessible. The shore and quay are now more defined, and boundaries are marked by low walls. Many elements are still visible, but the major change is to the station. The clock tower was removed along with the roof in 1978 and is no longer as imposing as it once was. The station is still important as it delivers many tourists who either stay at Lakeside and the Aquarium or continue their journey to Bowness and beyond by boat.

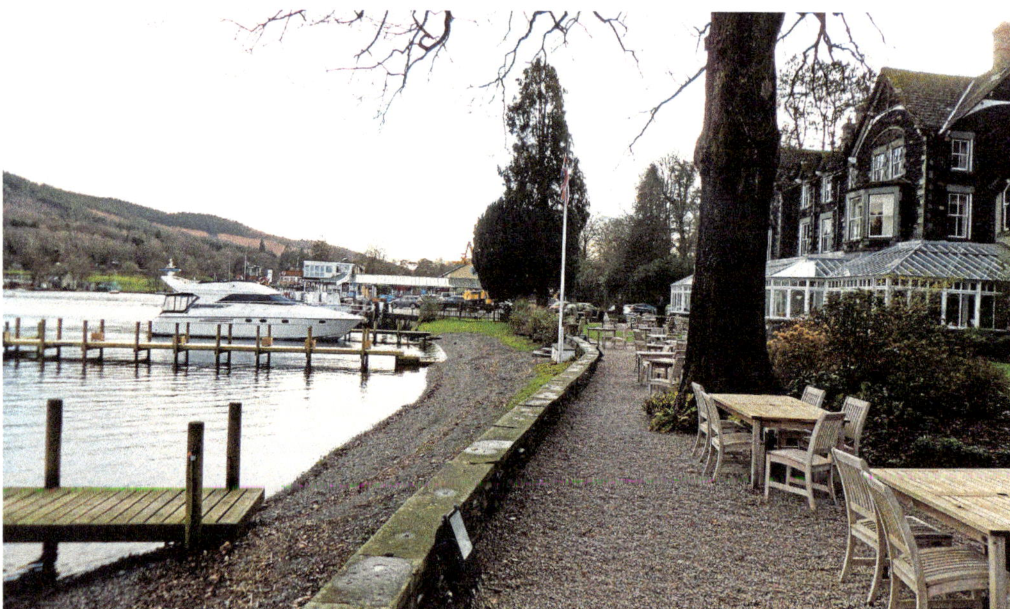

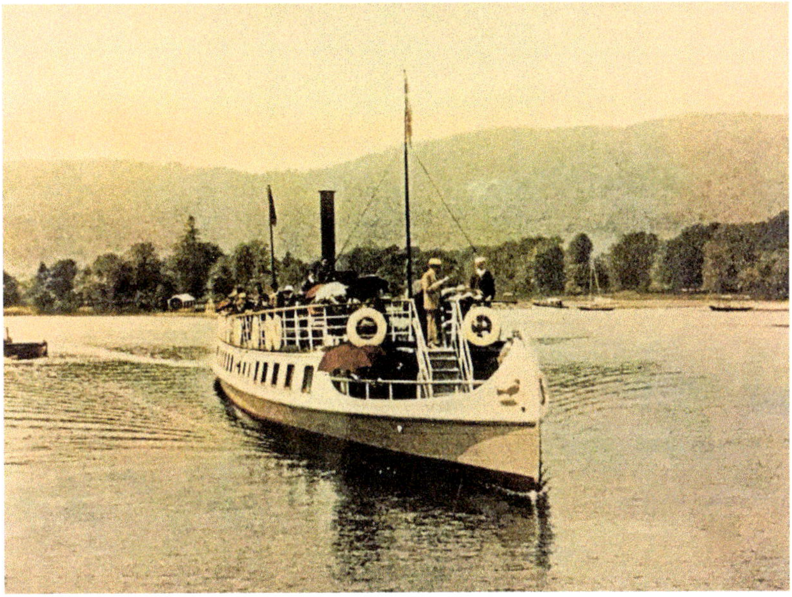

The Tern, Windermere

This pleasure boat was bought by the Furness Railway Co. in 1891 from Forrest and Sons of Wivenhoe. The steamship was principally used for excursions and was the largest vessel on Windermere when it was launched in 1891. The boat has undergone many changes over the years, the tall funnel replaced by a smaller one and diesel engines replacing the steam power. It is distinctive in shape, with a canoe bow. It was used as a training ship during the Second World War and bore the temporary name of HMS *Undine*. It has changed with the times but some of its original features were put back later. It can carry 350 passengers and has adapted to accommodate wheelchair users in accordance with modern requirements.

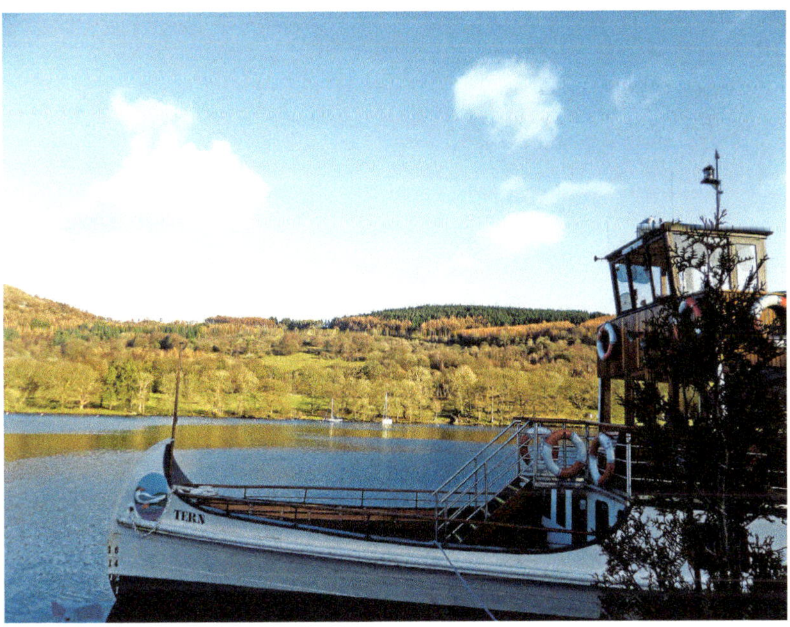

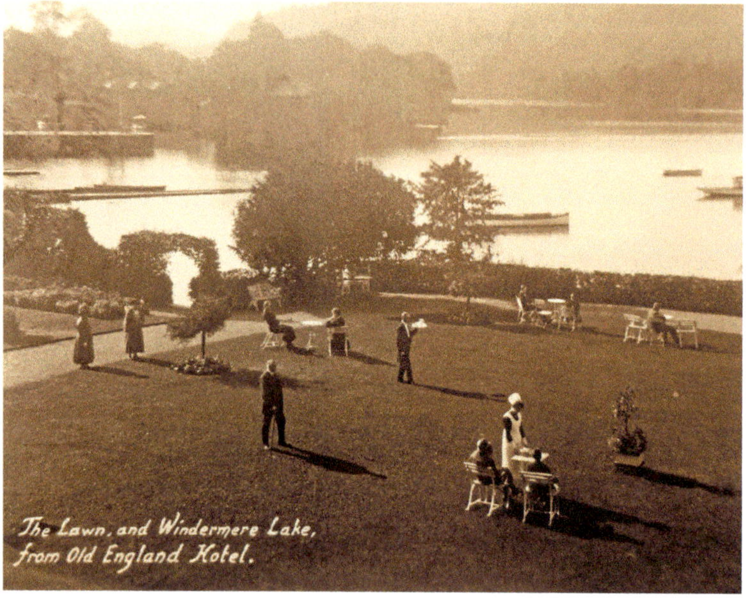

Old England Hotel Lawn

This photograph echoes a gentler and more elegant time which for those who love nostalgia has mostly gone. The lawn stretches down to the lakeside and in the distance the pleasure boats are moored. The people on the lawn are most likely to be residents of the hotel and presumably drawn from the middle class. People are having refreshments and it is surprising to us to see the waiter in tails and the waitress dressed in apron and cap. It is a charming snapshot of life between the wars and somewhat different to what we would see today. The lawn is still there, often used for photographs of weddings at the hotel, but maybe the view is intruded upon by more piers and more boats moored nearby. The hotel extensions have reduced the area of the lawn, but it is landscaped and is still a pleasant place to sit in the summer.

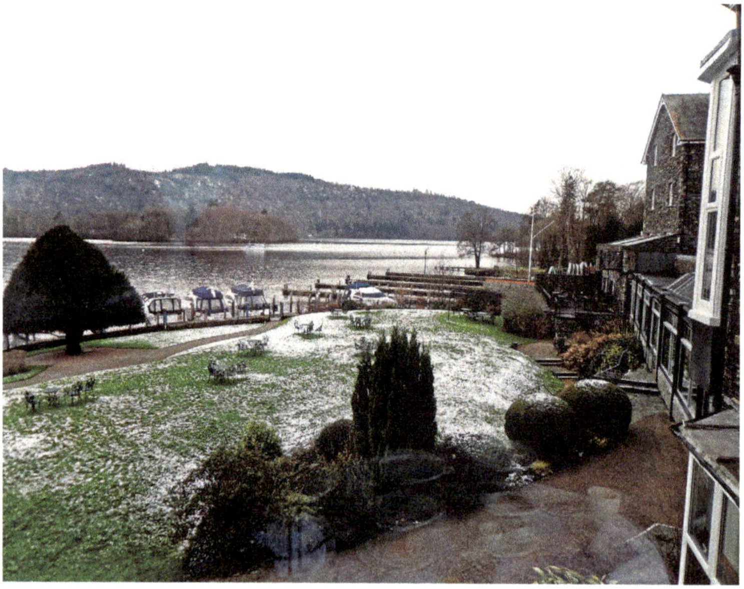

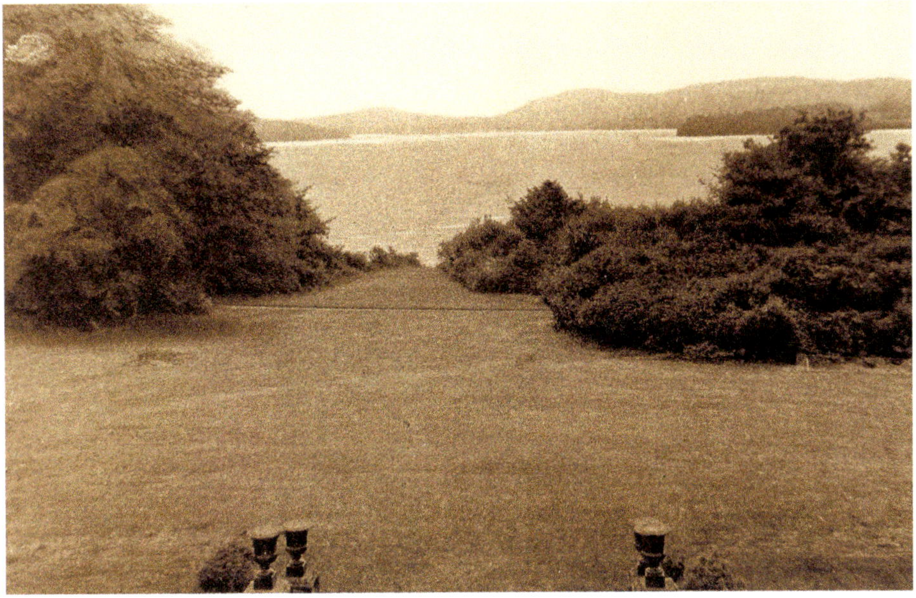

Storrs Hall Lawns, View to the Lake

With more than 17 acres of gardens to see the photograph only shows a small portion. The sweeping lawns stretch to the lakeside and the open views looking south are some of the best on Windermere. The view here is across the lake towards Claife Heights. The grounds allow access to the lakeside and there are beautiful woodland walks to be experienced. The stunning backdrop is an appropriate photographic opportunity for weddings and family occasions and is one of the enduring attractions of the hotel. There is now a boathouse for guests and a terrace, private jetty and even the room to accommodate a helicopter landing for those so inclined. A small gazebo adorns the lawn and a wide pathway to the lake edge and to the new cabins divides the view and provide access for visitors. An ornate urn can be seen in the picture. This could easily be one of those visible in the older photograph.

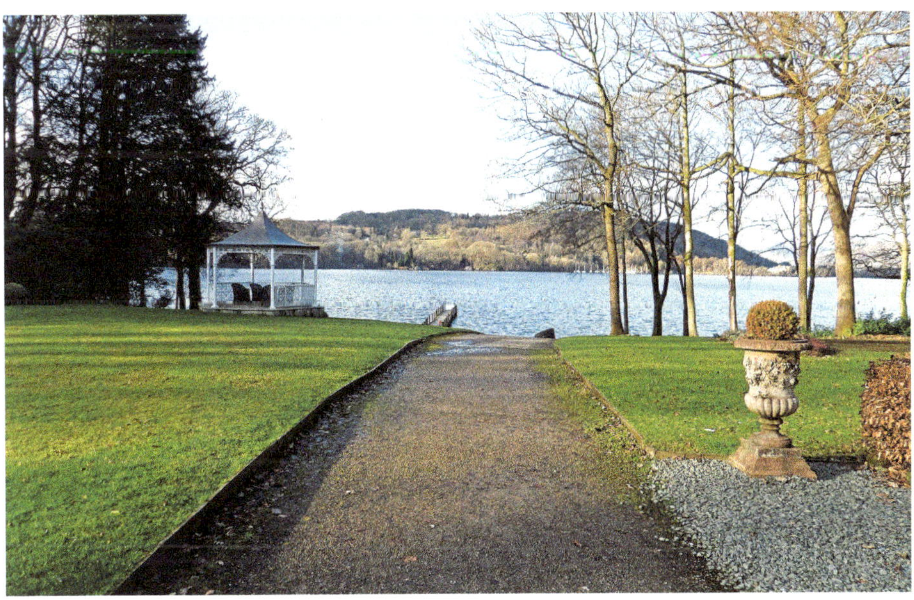

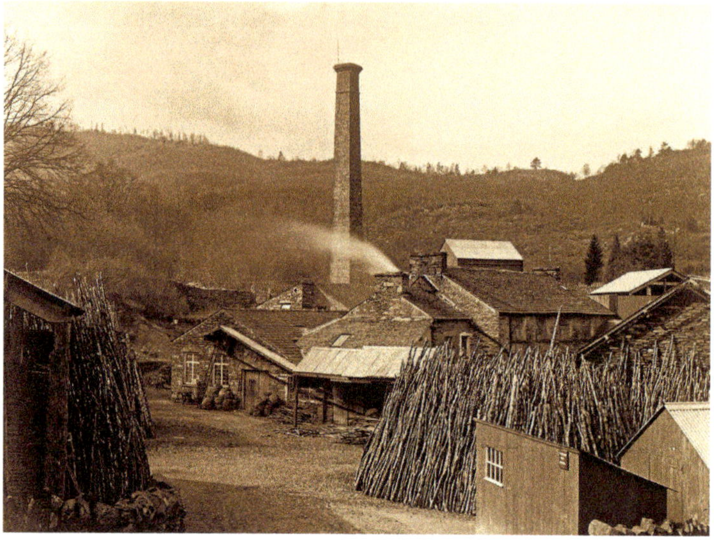

Stott Park Bobbin Mill

This remarkable building under the guardianship of English Heritage is the last working bobbin mill in the Lake District. Positioned close to Lake Windermere, it could take advantage of the natural resources on offer. It produced millions of wooden bobbins necessary for the Lancashire cotton mills. It employed around 250 men and boys, under often harsh conditions. The earliest mill was built in 1835 by John Harrison as a speculative venture, meeting the growing needs of industry, through several trustees. The Coward family leased it during the 1850s and expanded it, despite the difficulties arising from the cotton famine of the following decade. The advent of the railway helped its viability and it continued to thrive into the 1920s when the Cowards purchased the mill. Business continued until 1971 when the need for wooden bobbins fell and plastic became the material of choice. The steam engine that eventually superseded the waterwheel and turbine is still in working order and can be seen in action on special days. Bobbins are still produced, but now as a by-product of the tours and demonstrations. Outside is tidier than in its heyday, with picnic areas and heritage boards showing its new purpose as a visitor attraction. (Picture courtesy of English Heritage)

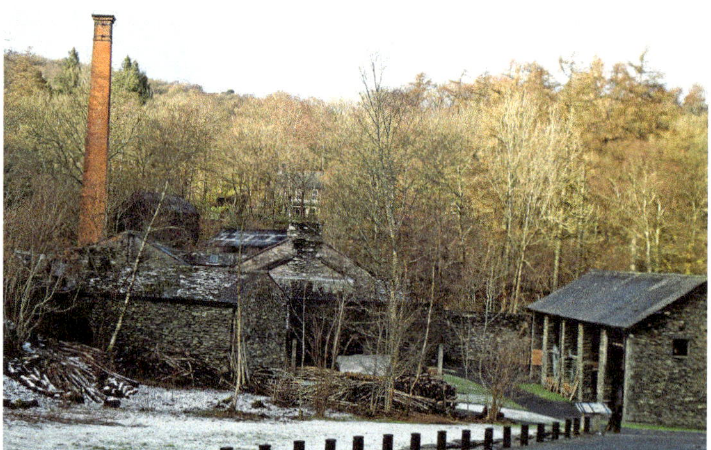

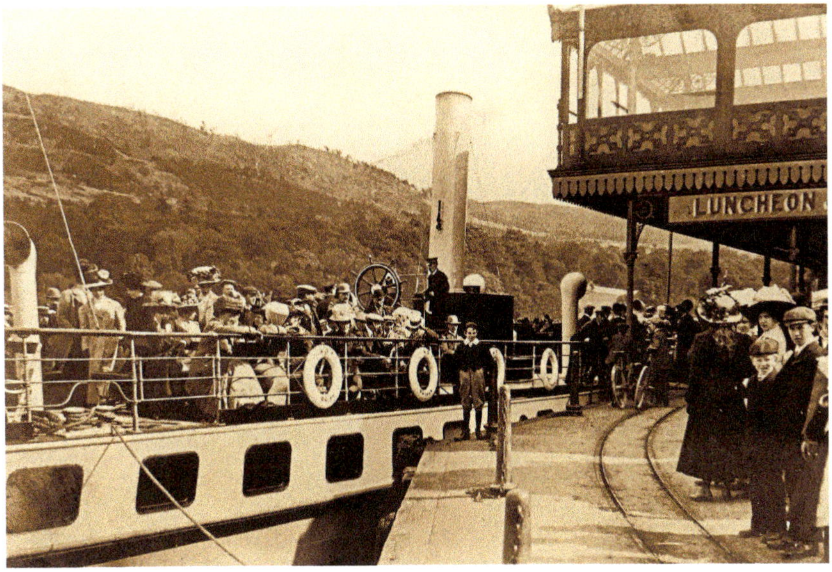

Lakeside Pier

This is a wonderful photograph taken at the height of summer – the dress of the visitors is cumbersome and probably their Sunday best. Excursions were a new phenomenon in Victorian times and it became a popular use of the limited free time available. By the time this picture was taken the tourist industry had taken off and the day trip was established as a holiday diversion. The long queue to the right can be easily replicated today (though maybe not as orderly) and the trips are still very popular. The refreshment Pavilion advertises 'luncheon', which sounds a rather posher affair than that available today. The modern picture is strangely devoid of passengers; this is because it was taken out of season. A similar picture in summer would be overwhelmed with families waiting to take the boat or use the café, shop and visit the aquarium.

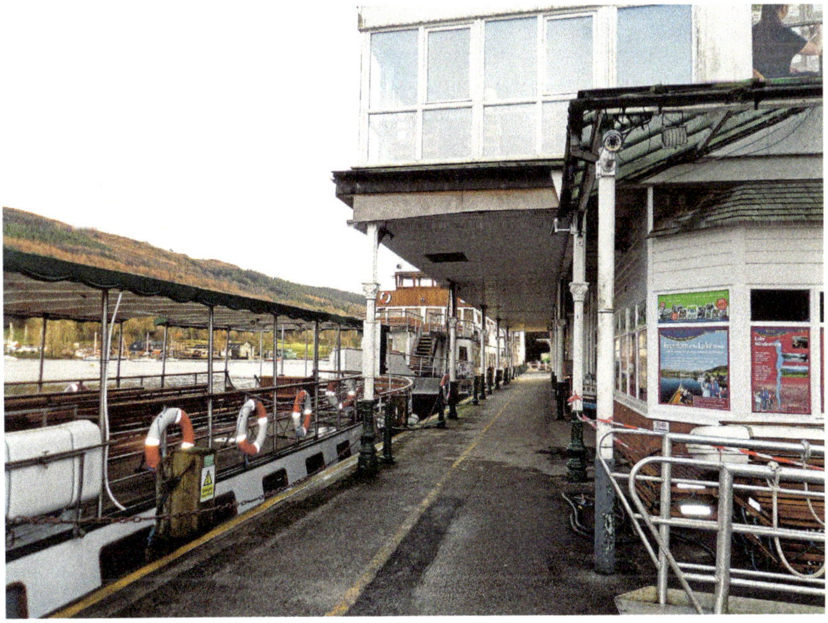

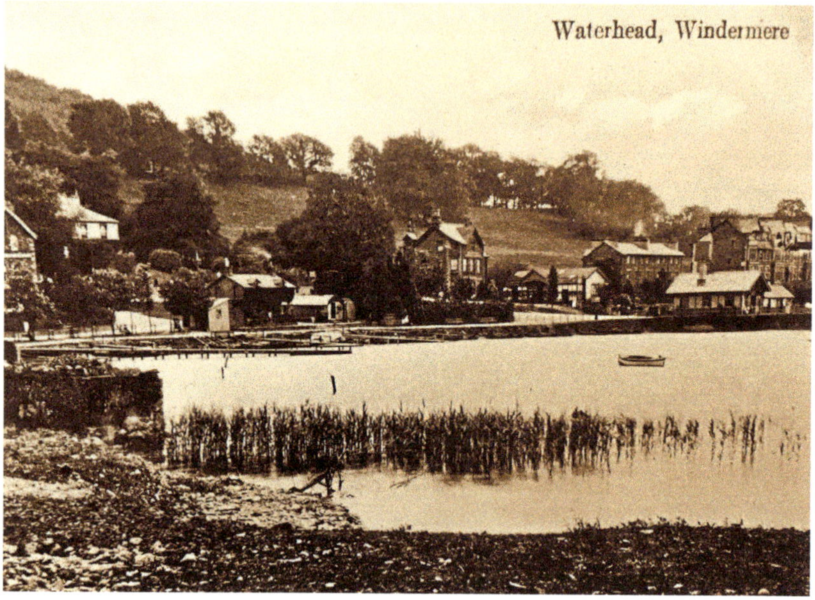

Waterhead, Windermere

At the other end of the lake is Waterhead, Ambleside. The view is similar today, though the number of buildings has increased. It has a pierhead for pleasure boats and an array of private jetties. The hotels have grown in number or have been extended and it is another popular place for visitors. The reed beds are still there but are further away from the piers. The visitors are deposited some distance from the centre of the village and a good walk is required to reach it. Borran's Road takes you through the back of Ambleside, past the Roman fort, avoiding the town and meandering through towards Coniston and Hawkshead. The A591 behind the hotels is the direct road into Ambleside and beyond. There are numerous pubs and hotels to visit from which to obtain the obligatory afternoon tea or for those with stronger tastes, a local ale.

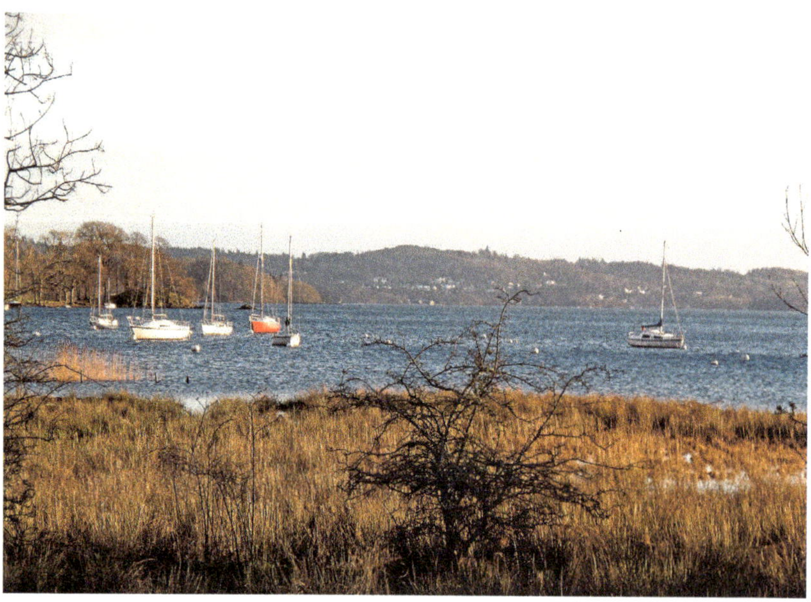

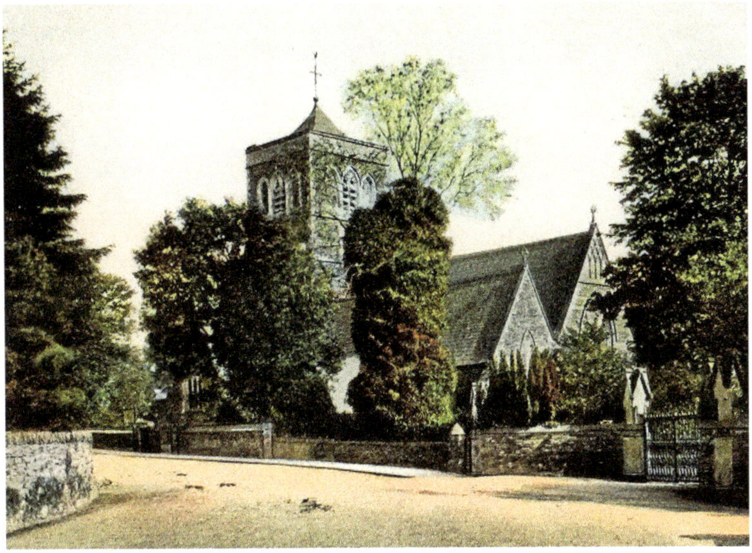

St Mary's Church, Windermere

This Grade II-listed building is an active Anglican church in Windermere. The original chapel was commissioned by Revd Addison in 1847. It seems strange to us that the vicar would build his own church, but this is exactly what happened. The church was a simple style to begin with but in 1852 the south aisle was added. In 1855 Addison sold the church to the village due to personal financial issues and the church became the parish church for Windermere. Further additions and extensions were made over the years, and Paley and Austin restored the church adding a chancel and vestry. A central tower was added later and little of the original church remained. The church has continually been subjected to alterations and the reredos installed by Paley and Austin was removed in 1945. A fire destroyed the nave roof in 1988 and was restored in the coming years. Modernisation and partitioning took place in 2005–06 bringing it into line with many other old churches, to give usable spaces, kitchen and a refreshment area for the modern congregation. Externally, it is similar to the first picture and it is surrounded by a peaceful graveyard lined with trees.

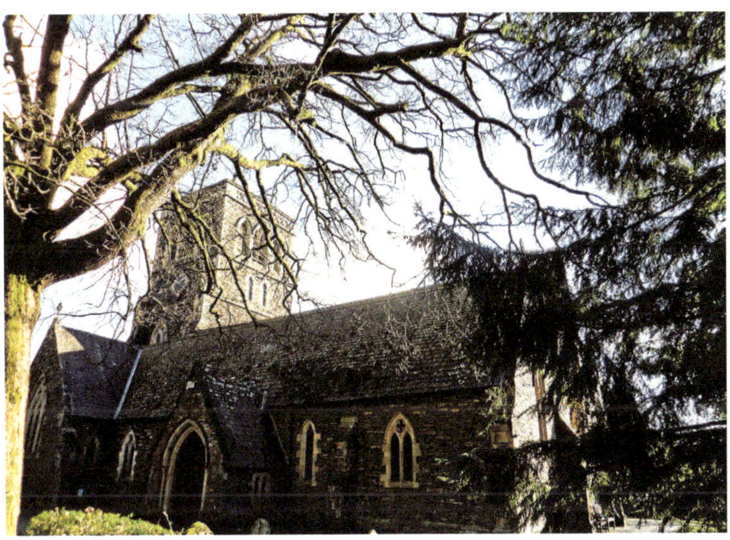

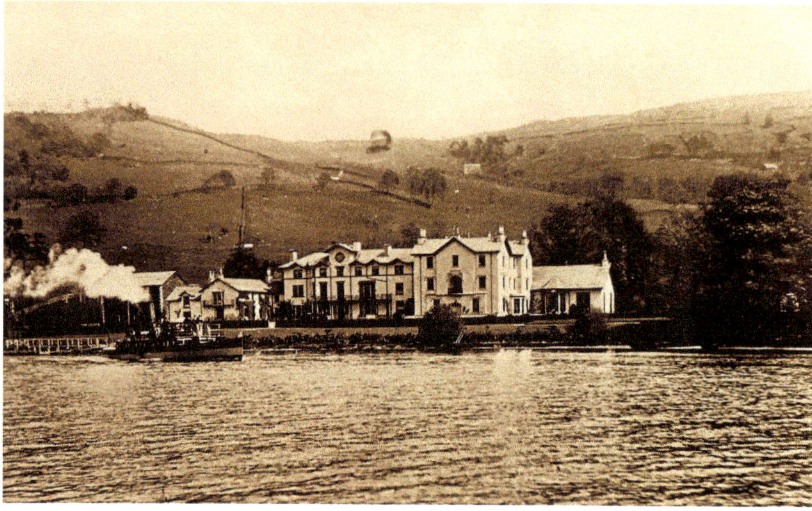

Low Wood, Windermere

This well-known and imposing hotel has a longer history than one might expect. It started life as a farm which became a small hostelry for travellers in the eighteenth century. The Lake District then was a more dangerous place in which to travel, with poor roads, robbers and extreme weather, so one can see why this building is well placed as a safe haven. A new turnpike road was opened in the 1760s bringing travellers from Kendal to Keswick. This heralded the start of tours to the Lakes and tourism as we know it grew from these humble beginnings. Its first mention in travel guides was in 1825 when John Briggs recorded the excellence of the puddings at the hostelry. In the following years people like Wordsworth, Ruskin and Turner visited, placing it firmly on the map. The Logan family ran the hotel from 1845 for ninety years, developing it into an attractive and sought-after destination. Norman Buckley, the next owner, made it the largest hotel in the Lake District with 140 rooms. It has again been extended and refurbished from 2017 in a £16 million project, which will include the obligatory spa, sauna, fitness suite and heated pool according to the promotional material, making it the Lake District's 'first world-class luxury resort'.

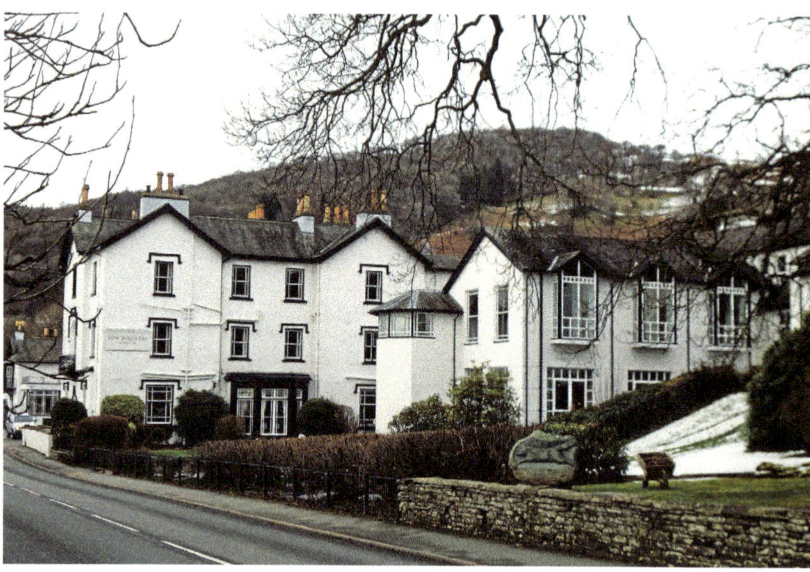

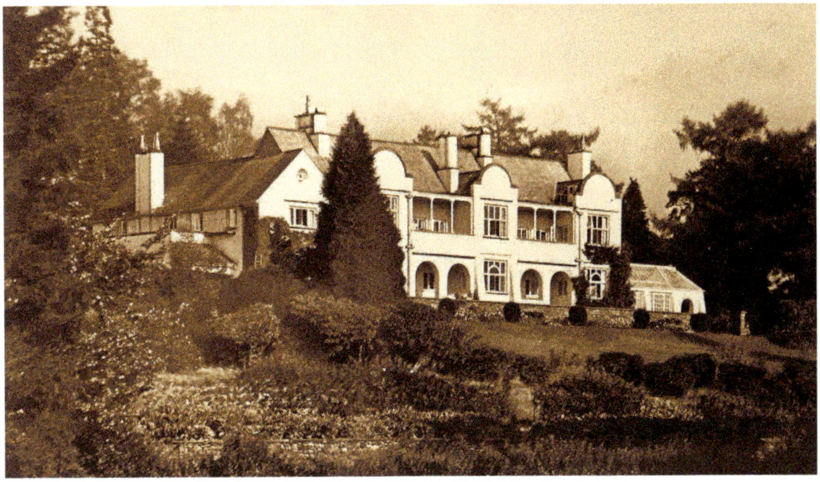

Brockhole

This imposing Victorian villa was built in 1897 by William Henry Adolphus Gaddum. He was a rich silk merchant operating from Manchester and he required a summer residence which suited his position in society. The Lake District had become a popular choice for the nouveaux riche; manufacturers, industrialists, business men who wanted to display their wealth all converged on the fashionable Lakes, just as Wordsworth had predicted. Many of these private mansions littered the edge of Lake Windermere and attracted many famous visitors, such as Beatrix Potter and her family. She mentions her numerous visits to Brockhole in her diaries and was very familiar with the area. After William Gaddum died the house was sold, becoming a convalescent home run by the Merseyside Hospital Board. In 1966 the house and grounds were bought by the Lake District National Park Authority and later became a visitor centre. The gardens are of special note, being designed by Thomas Mawson, who was responsible for those at Blackwell and Rydal Mount as well. Brockhole has been a popular tourist destination ever since and has been conserved and renovated through the years. The views are spectacular, and steamers travel to the pier at Brockhole in the summer months.

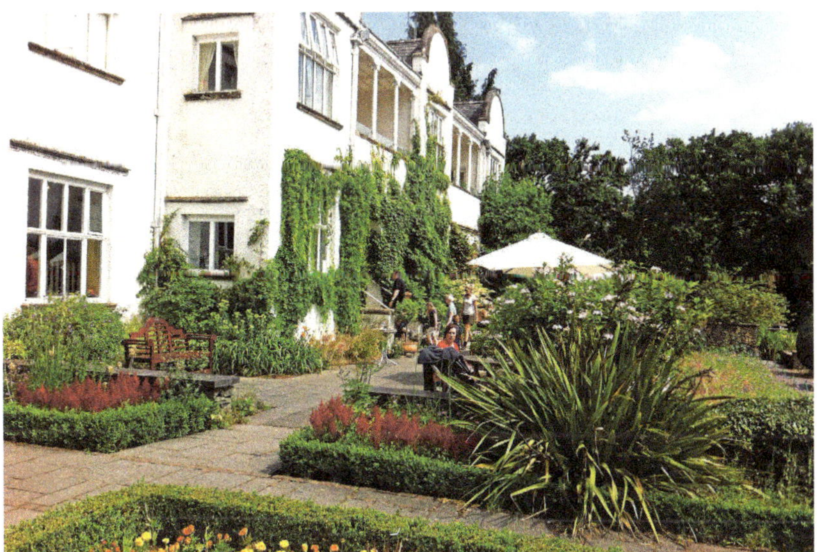

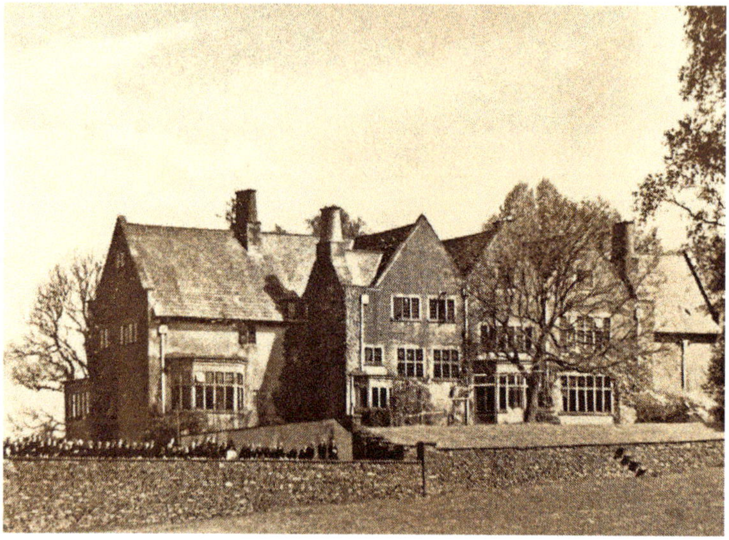

Blackwell

M. H. Baillie Scott designed this Arts and Crafts house between 1897 and 1900 for Sir Edward Holt, a brewer from Manchester. Heavily influenced by Ruskin and Morris, the Arts and Crafts movement was a response to industrialisation and mass production. This house is a remarkable example of the style and has many examples of furniture and objects designed by Baillie Scott. The original features have survived and are breathtakingly beautiful, whether it is the hand-crafted tiles, furniture, the wooden decoration, stained glass or the inglenook fireplaces. It has a fairy-tale feel and the views over the lake and gardens enhance this. The gardens were designed by Thomas Mawson in attractive terraces around the house, filled with herbs and flowers. The house was turned into a school in 1941 by Huyton College to allow their younger pupils to be evacuated from the bombing in Liverpool. The headmistress, Miss Murphy, seems to have resonated with the creativity of the building and the girls were treated to exciting outdoor activities including ice skating and fell walking. The house continued to be used as a prep school until 1962 and closed as a school in 1972. The house is run by the Lakeland Arts Trust and has been open to the public since 2001. The view is relatively unchanged.

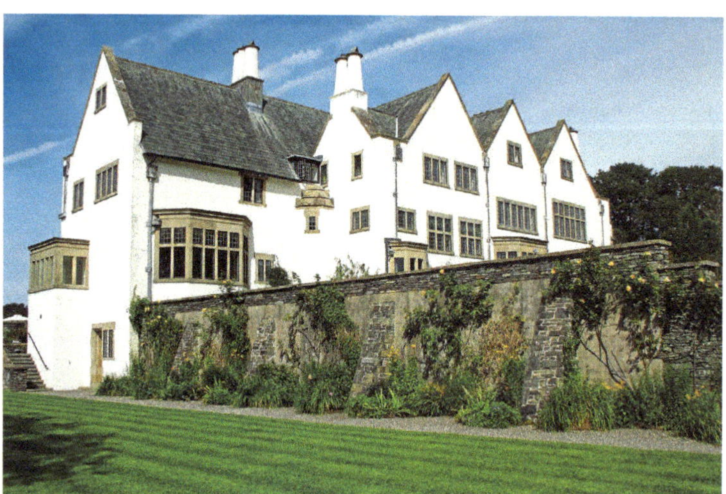

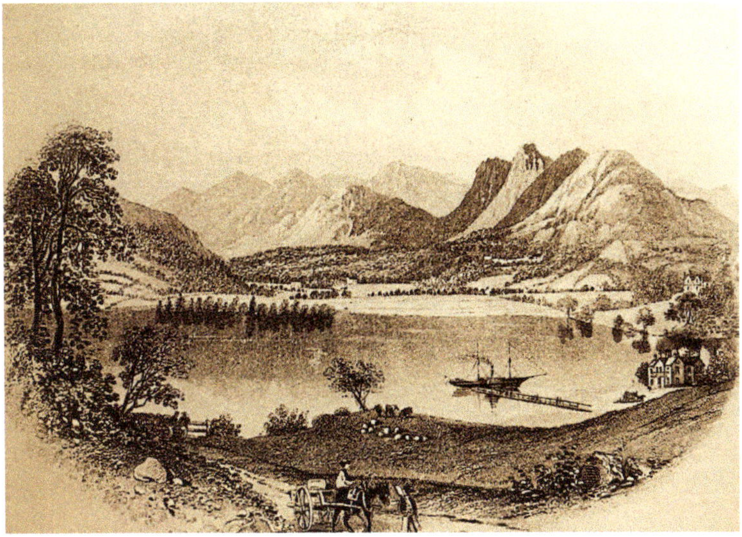

Windermere

The old sketch of Windermere is very dramatic and sums up the accepted image of the Lake District. The elements that first attracted visitors to explore this wild region in the eighteenth and nineteenth century are all there: high mountains, large tracts of water, rurality, boats and nature in abundance. This view has been perpetuated ever since and while it fits with the Romantic perspective, it is still what many people are seeking when they venture into the Lakes. The modern picture taken at Lakeside still reflects those ideals, but we can't help but notice the slick and smart nature of the boats. They are no longer purely functional; now they are part status symbol, part sporting image – the 'active' lakes. The experience is the same as the early visitors had, but more so. All aspects are still present, the beauty and scenery unchanged, the experiences ever more challenging, exciting or colourful. The lake is in many places a manicured and controlled environment, still beautiful but in many ways enhanced and magnified in the same ways the hotels have been, a sort of 'boutique' lake.

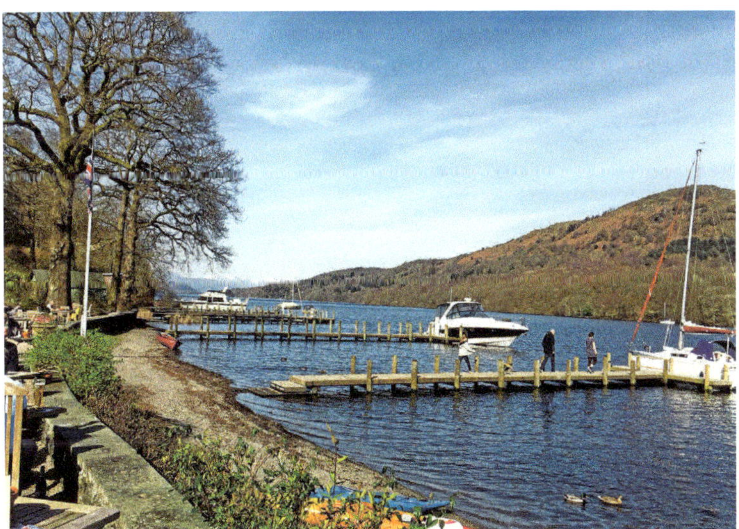

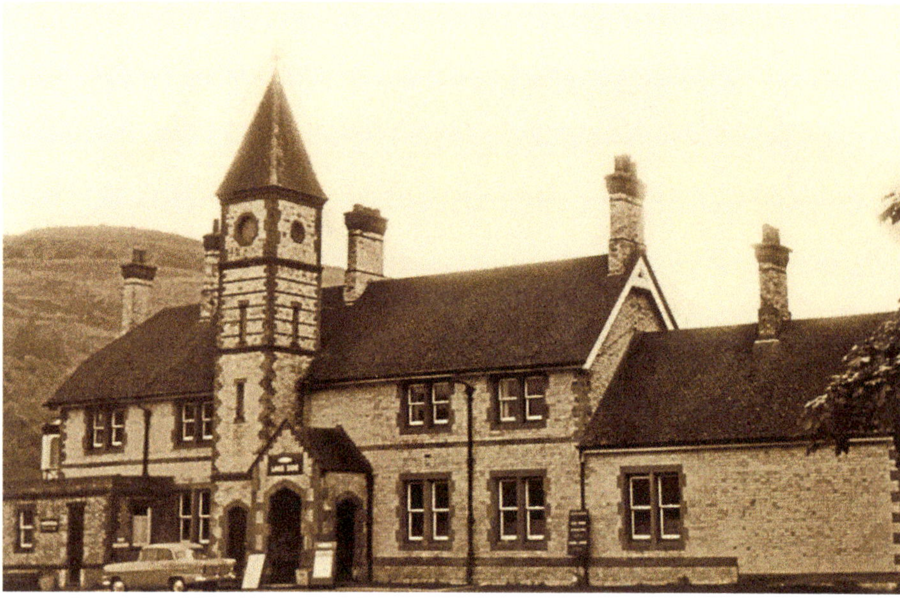

Lakeside Railway Station

Lakeside railway station was originally built as an extension from Ulverston to Newby Bridge in 1872. Furness Railway bought the Windermere Steam Ferry and were able to coordinate the two services, which would prove to be a very popular tourist destination. It was closed in 1965 under the Beeching cuts. It soon became derelict and for safety purposes the clock tower and roof were removed in 1978. This changed the appearance of the building irrevocably. The current building is less impressive and certainly less attractive, but serves its purpose. Trains began running again in 1973 from Haverthwaite and have proved to be very popular. The new Heritage line appeals to steam enthusiasts and at certain times of the year special excursions are put on, the most popular being the Santa train ride in December. The ferry service still connects with the train service but is a separate concern. The Lakes Aquarium now stands beside the station and is another addition to the tourist offer.

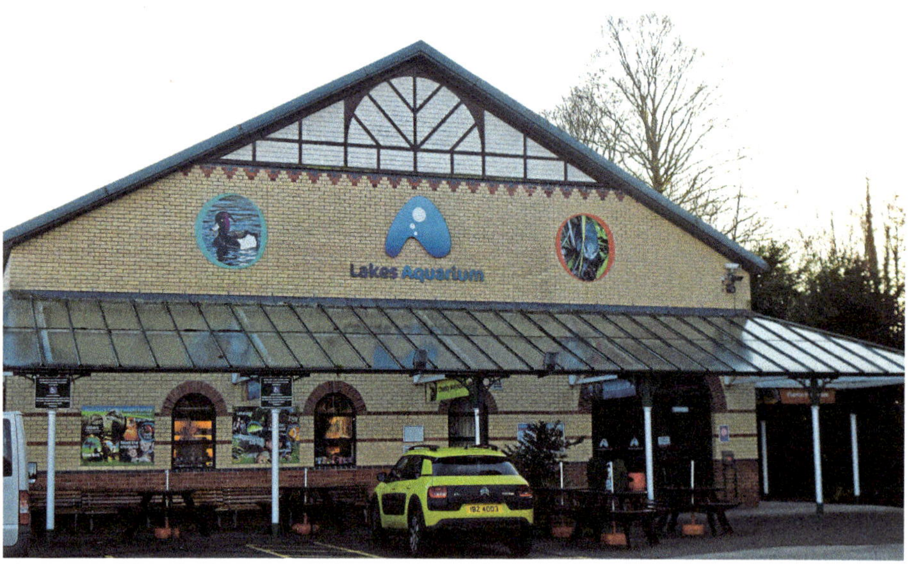

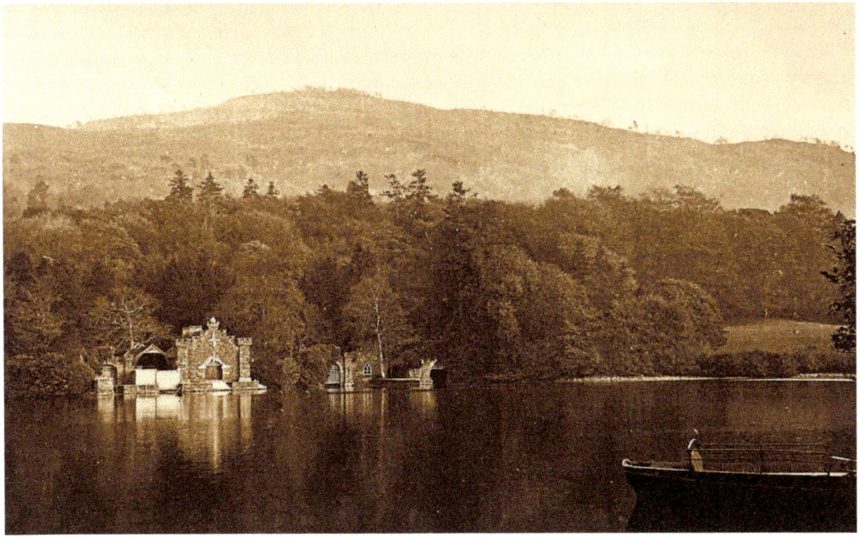

Fell Foot, Newby Bridge

This park is a very popular destination for both tourists and local people, particularly in the summer. The National Trust provide events and activities for both children and adults, such as the Park Run, which has a good following. The park is a place of beauty and safety for children, allowing them the chance to access the lake and the grounds. There is a café and a shop in what were the boathouses, which are two of the only buildings left from the original estate. There are water sports and boat rides available and the National Trust rangers provide many activities. In summer the park can be very crowded and busy, but there is something quite satisfying in seeing all the different families enjoying the countryside. Fell Foot is another place that has suffered from flooding in recent years. Naturally, the boathouses are susceptible to the floods because they were originally meant to be open to the water, but the lake has broken its banks on more than one occasion and extensive flooding has occurred right down as far as the Swan at Newby Bridge. (Photo courtesy of National Trust)

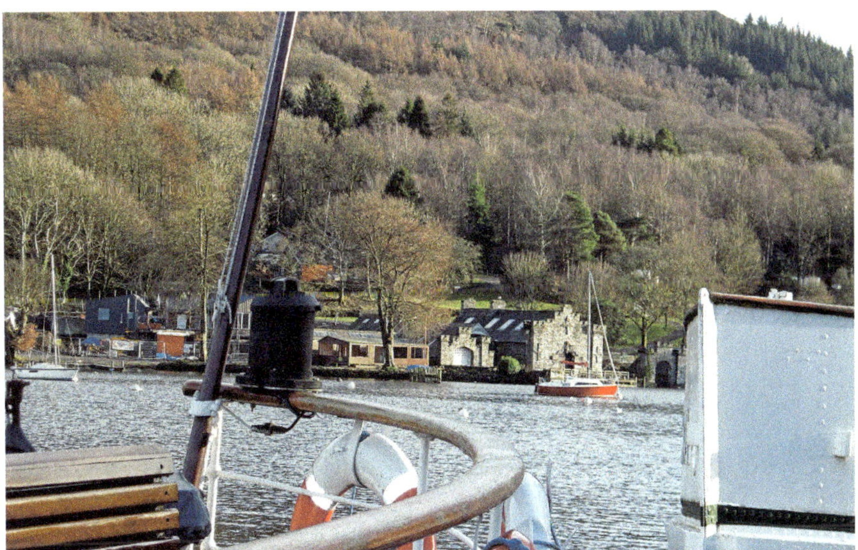

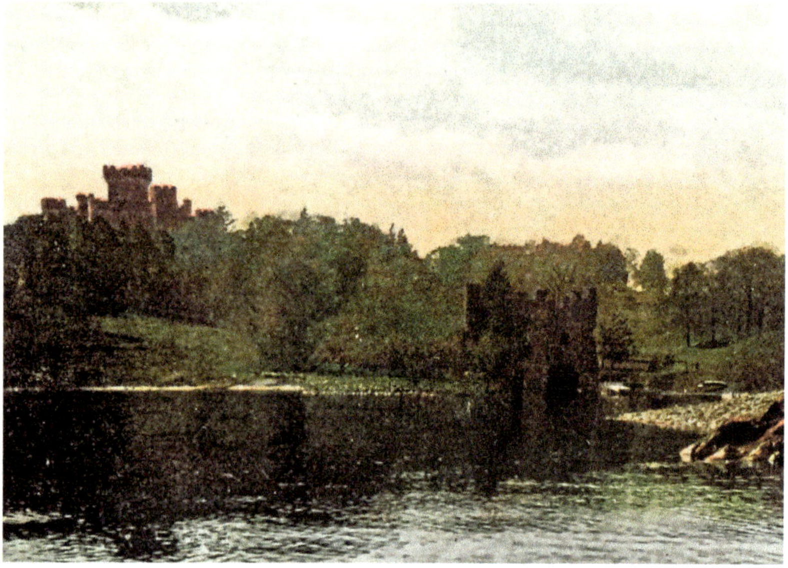

Wray Castle

Yet another grand house built by an 'offcomer', Wray is a grand neo-Gothic Victorian edifice built in 1840 by James Dawson and his wife Margaret. Dawson was a surgeon from Liverpool who funded this project with his wife's inheritance from the gin industry. It is an enormous Victorian folly, which Dawson's wife allegedly refused to live in. It was a grandiose scheme which presents as a faux medieval castle; on first appraisal it is most convincing. The interest in the house arises from the association with both later owners and famous visitors. Dawson's young nephew inherited the property in 1875. Two years later his cousin Hardwicke Rawnsley was appointed vicar of Wray church. Rawnsley was a follower of Ruskin and a founder member of the National Trust. Interestingly, Beatrix Potter, who was also a founder member, had stayed at the castle as a young girl with her parents for six weeks. This was probably one of the holidays to the Lakes which inspired her to return and put down her own roots. (Photo courtesy of Harriet Baxter)

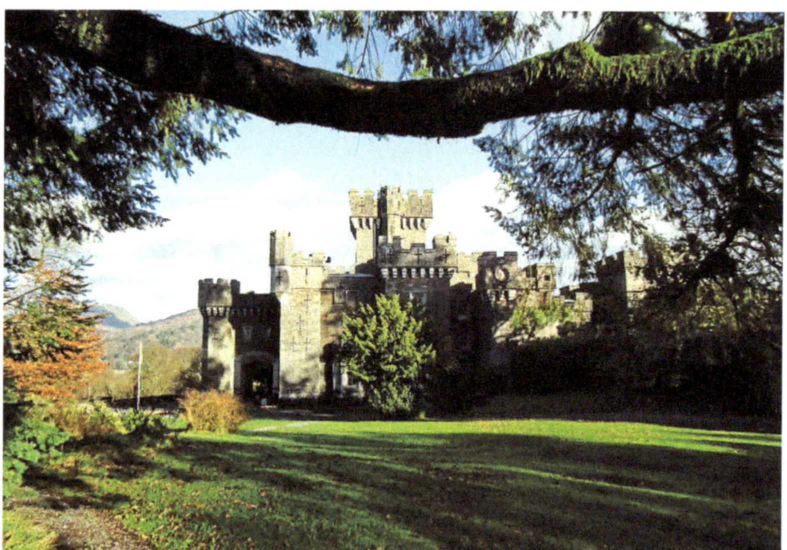

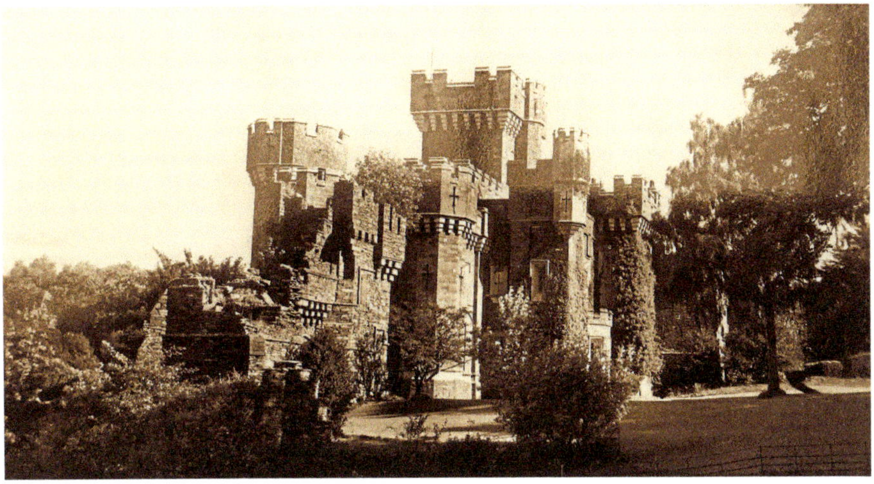

Wray Castle

The castle was acquired by the National Trust in 1929 and became a youth hostel. In the 1930s it was used by the Freshwater Biological Association, which was appropriate given its position next to the lake. Later in 1958 it became a training facility for merchant seamen (RMS Wray Castle). In 2004 this ceased due to technological changes in the navy and the building was no longer required. The Trust have converted the empty castle into a visitor attraction, principally focused on children. This has close links with Beatrix Potter and Peter Rabbit and has provided a lucrative solution for the Trust. There are mixed reviews on this use of the heritage property: families seem to love it as it is geared towards pleasing children; adults, who are perhaps unaware of the nature of the attraction before they visit, are surprised by the absence of furnishings and interior décor and are disappointed at the lack of 'history'. However, the gardens and the views make up for this somewhat. (Photo courtesy Harriet Baxter)

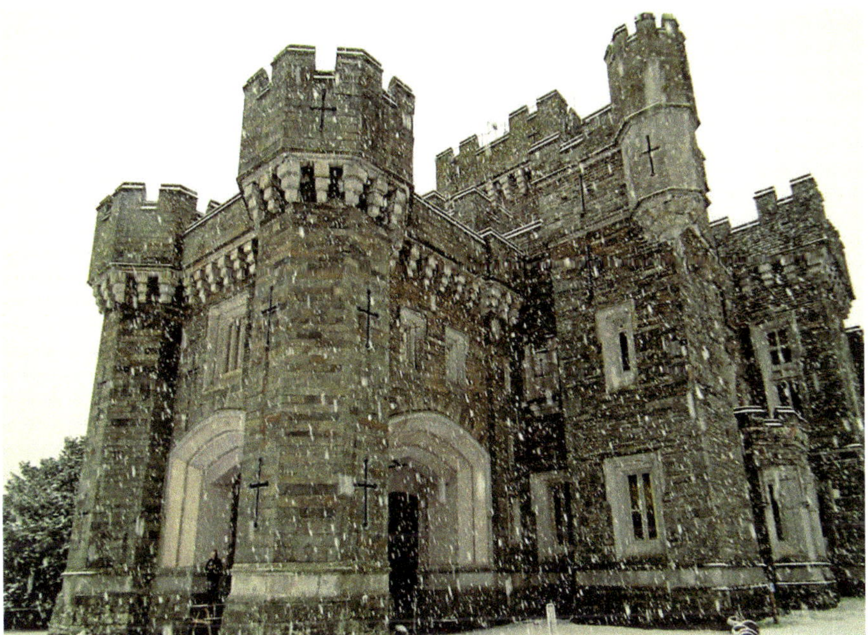

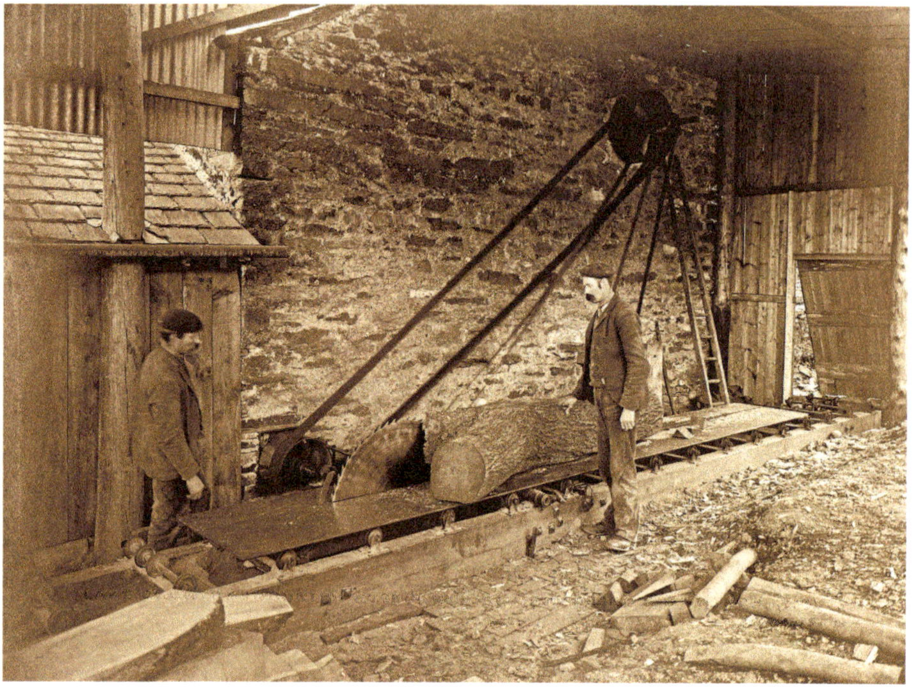

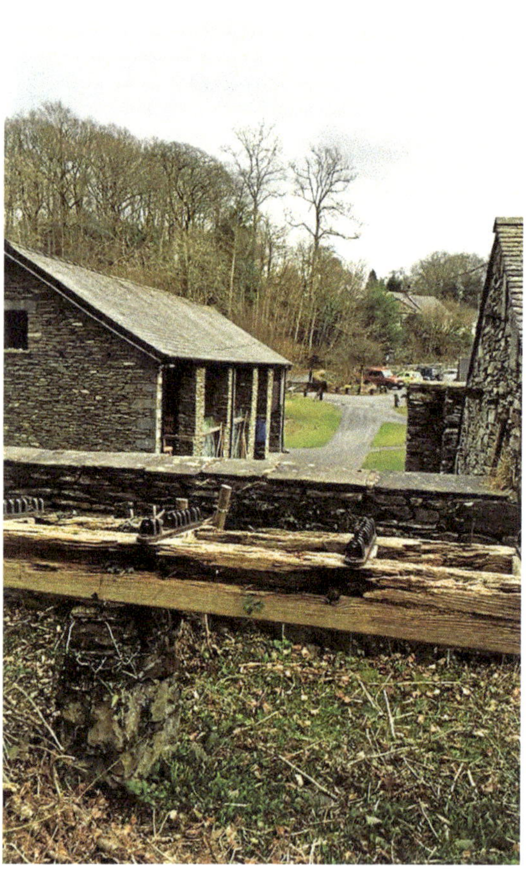

Travelling Saw Bench, Stott Park Mill

This lethal-looking piece of machinery is a travelling saw bench. The picture dates form 1909 and is a James Atkinson (Ulverston) print. The men in the photo are dressed in working clothes, but with no protective clothing other than sturdy clogs on their feet. The massive saw was used to cut the coppiced wood into workable lengths. There is a roller system beneath to allow them to move the wood easily and there is a hatch at the end of the shed. As you would expect at this time there are no health and safety guards on either the saw or the pulleys and leather bands. Work in a saw mill could be dangerous and required care and skill to operate safely. The modern view is of a piece of the infrastructure of the mill removed as part of conservation and the drying sheds to the left and mill to the right. (Photo courtesy of English Heritage, Stott Park)

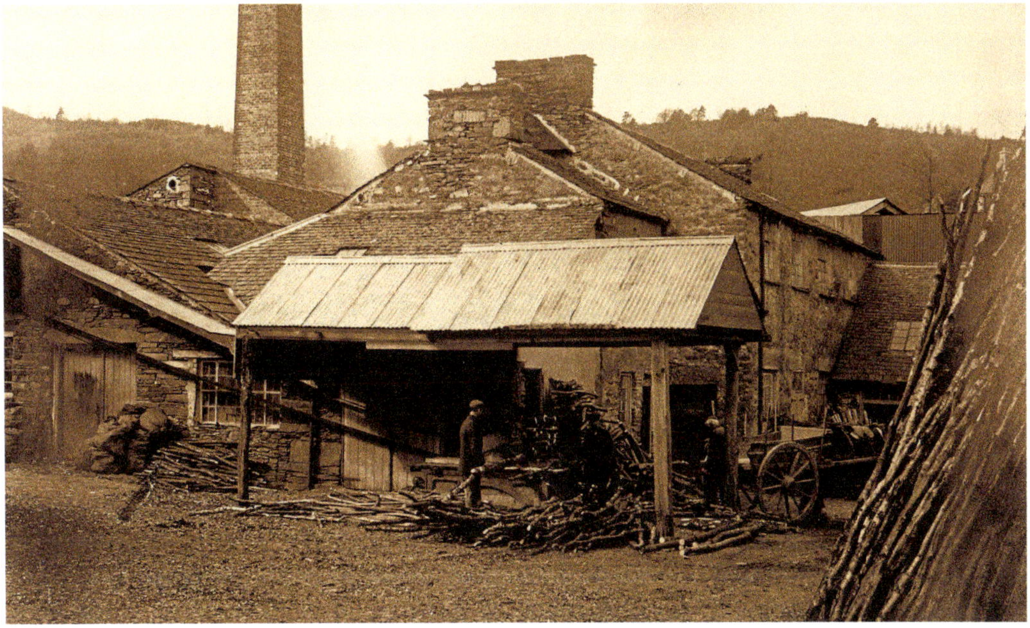

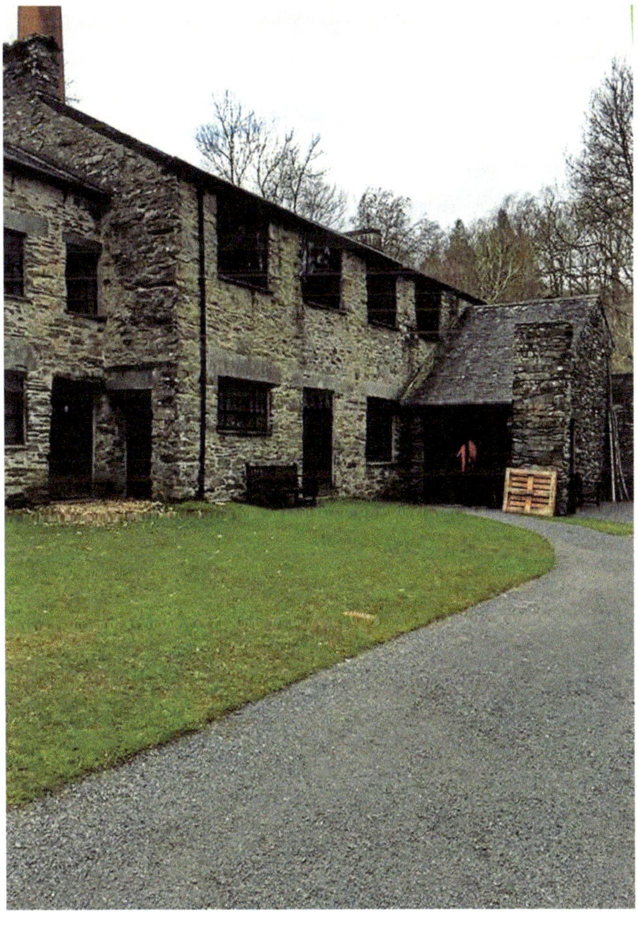

Making Cross Cutting, Stott Park

Another hazardous job is being undertaken in this Atkinson picture. The men are using a saw to cut the lengths of wood across the trunk. The process of preparation of the coppiced trunks was lengthy and sometimes hazardous. The lack of personal protective clothing is starkly obvious to us, and this process would have contributed to poor safety and risk of injury. The sanitised view of the heritage establishment is a far cry from the reality of the gruelling conditions endured by workers in 1909. When demonstrating some of the tasks the present English Heritage staff have proper clothing and safety guards on machinery, a luxury not afforded to their predecessors. (Photo courtesy of English Heritage, Stott Park)

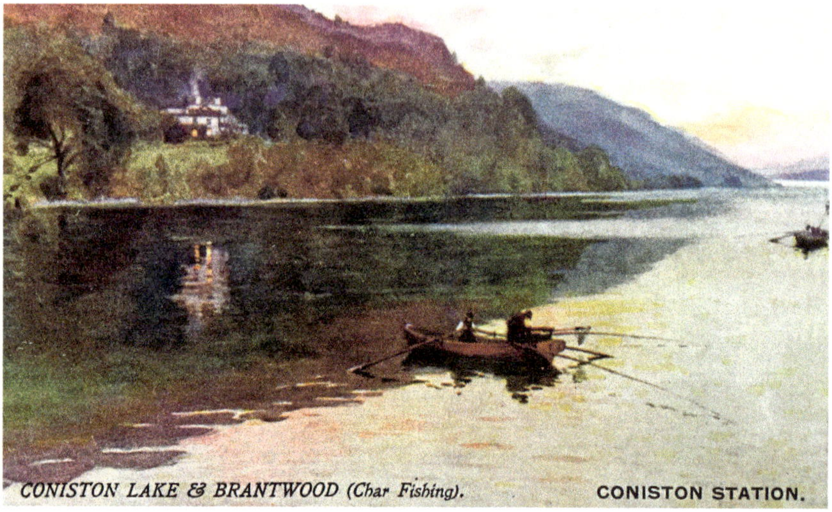

Brantwood from Across the Lake

In 1871 Brantwood was sold to John Ruskin, who allegedly bought it unseen. Ruskin arranged for extensive repairs to the house, as well as additional building – such as a turret room, which revealed amazing views up and down the lake – for his personal use. The lodge was built for his valet and there was a coach house, a stable and even an ice house. Major improvements to the garden were made and he was enthusiastic about horticulture and conservation. Its style is Arts and Crafts as one would expect, and it holds an imposing position, visible from the village across the lake. The views from Brantwood are spectacular and show Coniston Old Man in its ever-changing glory. As in Ruskin's day the house is filled with art and beauty and classes and tutorials are held regularly. It was extended again when the Severns came to live at Brantwood, a studio being added to accommodate Arthur Severn who was an artist. After Severn's death in 1931 the estate was sold, and the contents dispersed. The house was rescued from impending obscurity by John Howard Whitehouse, founder of Bembridge School and the Birmingham Ruskin Society, who bought it. He established the Brantwood Trust in 1951 and the Trust still administers the house and conserves Ruskin's legacy.

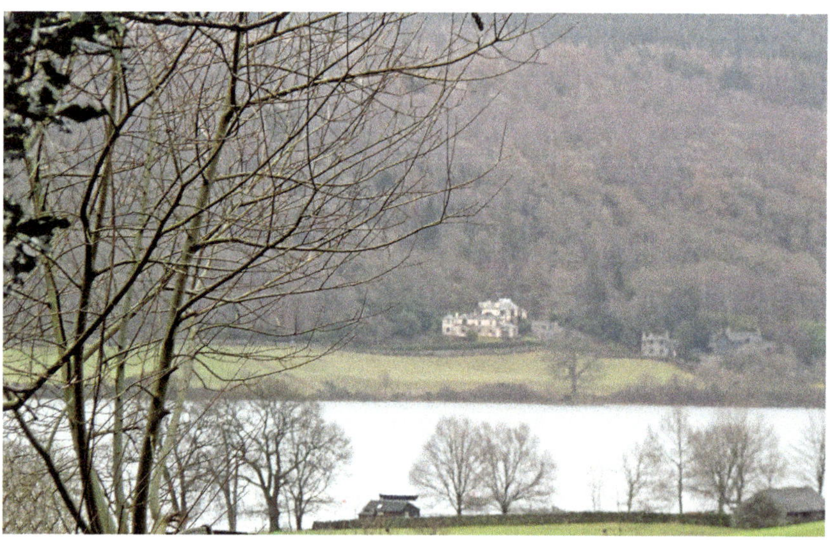

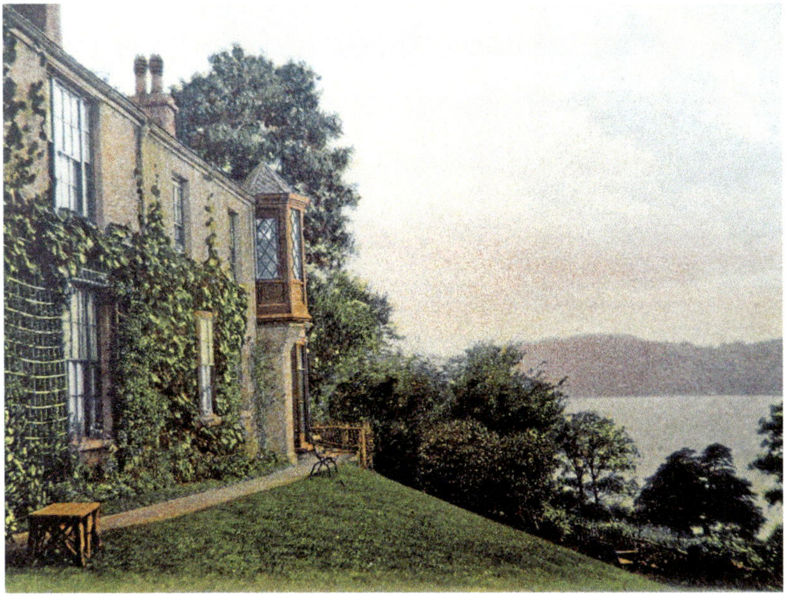

Brantwood, Coniston

The Brantwood Trust administer the home of Ruskin and it is now a Grade II-listed building. When Ruskin died in 1900 he made provision for the house to be open to the public for thirty days a year so that his vast collection of art could be seen. Unfortunately, the Severn family who inherited the house failed to do this and sold numerous pictures and furnishings. In Ruskin's time, as can be imagined, the house was a magnet for artists and writers. Frequent visitors included W. G. Collingwood, Canon Rawnsley and many more. The house has been restored and some of the original furniture and artwork is on display again. It has become a popular tourist destination and the gardens have been restored to their former glory. Brantwood holds many art events throughout the year and has an artist in residence post. The 'Friends of Ruskin' volunteer and raise funds to help maintain this prominent place.

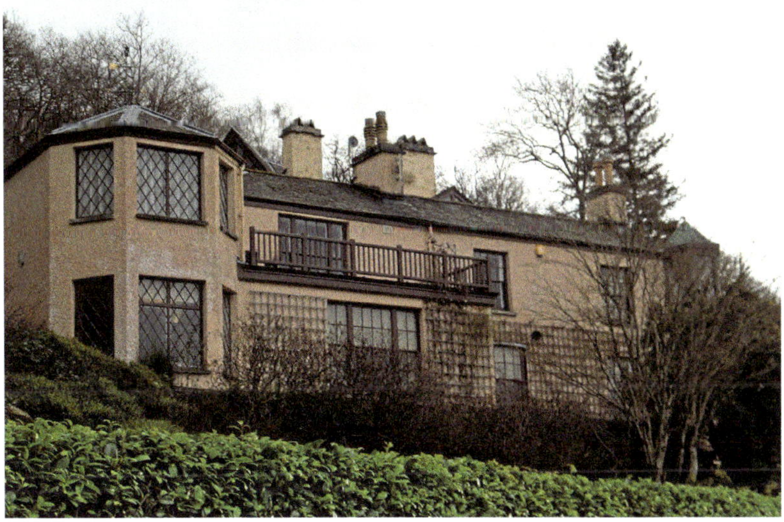

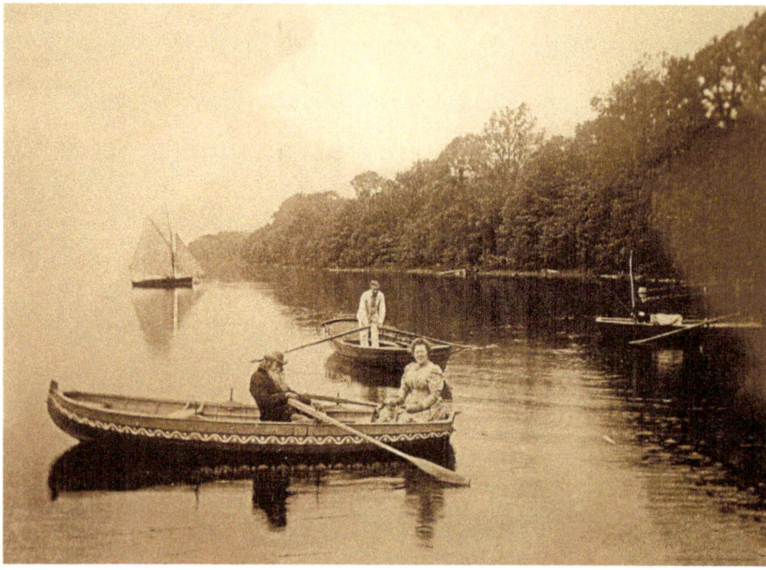

John Ruskin, Coniston Water

This picture is from our family collection. My great-grandfather Miles Wilkinson was Ruskin's last head gardener. We have assorted items such as this from his time there. The photograph shows Ruskin as an old man, rowing Joan Severn, his cousin. The man in the other boat is possibly her husband, Arthur Severn. The Severns, as his closest living relatives, inherited Brantwood from Ruskin. The lake was accessed through the lower gardens and there is still a jetty to allow boats to be moored. The Severn family lived both at Brantwood and in their London home at Warwick Square. In the 1930s, after Arthur Severn died, the estate was sold off and many of the items from the house were bought by local people and those who had worked at Brantwood. Some of these have been donated back to the house in later years and are exhibited there now. The Gondola steam boat docks at the Brantwood pier as part of a circular tour on the lake. (Picture courtesy of Margaret Thwaites)

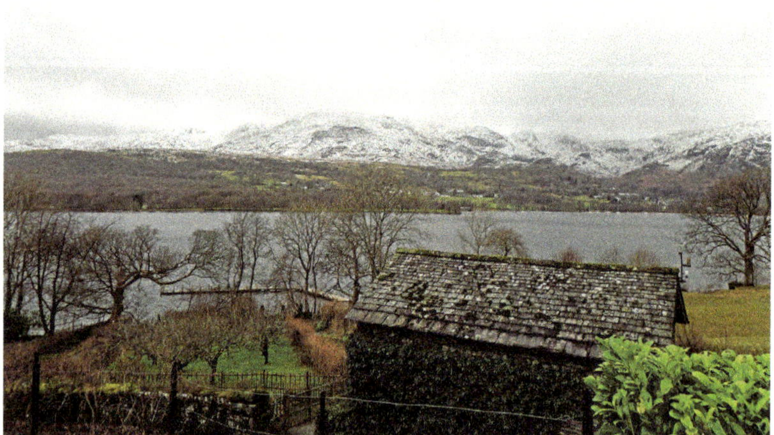

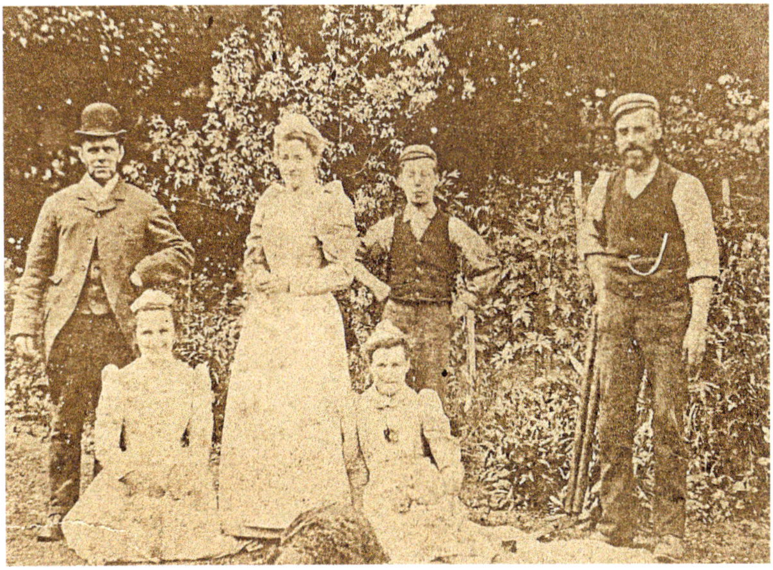

Brantwood Staff and the Lodge

Miles Wilkinson learnt the trade at Brantwood under the then head gardener Herdson and procured references from Professor Ruskin to take up work elsewhere to develop his skills. He returned to Brantwood and became gardener and then later head gardener. He continued to work there after Ruskin's death for the Severns and he died at the Lodge at Brantwood in April 1920. The death was sudden, and Arthur Severn wrote a letter to *The Times* apologising for his absence at the funeral. The photograph shows him with the staff from Brantwood, some of whom are unnamed – Miles is far right with the beard and the gentleman on the far left is possibly 'Chadwick'. Sadly, there is some confusion about his position and he is often misidentified as his brother Joe, who was the coachman at this time rather than the gardener. The Lodge is now a holiday home which has been renovated to provide comfortable accommodation for those who wish to spend time at Ruskin's home. (Picture courtesy of Margaret Thwaites)

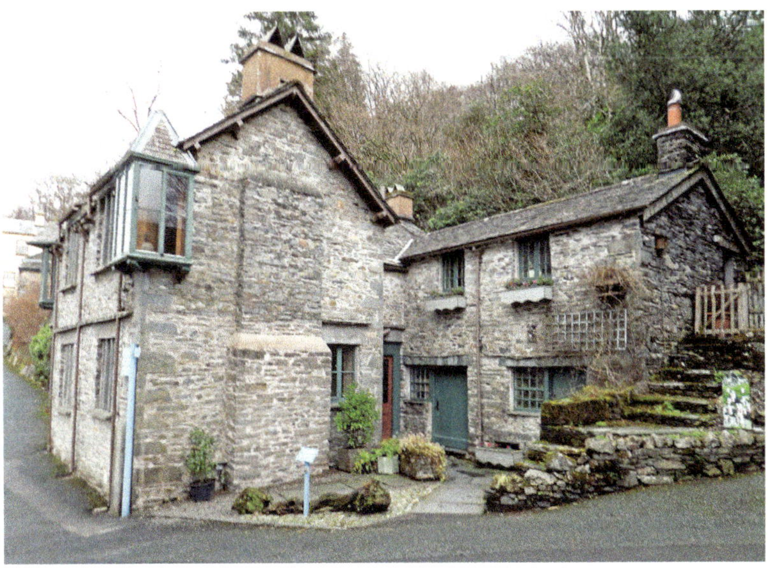

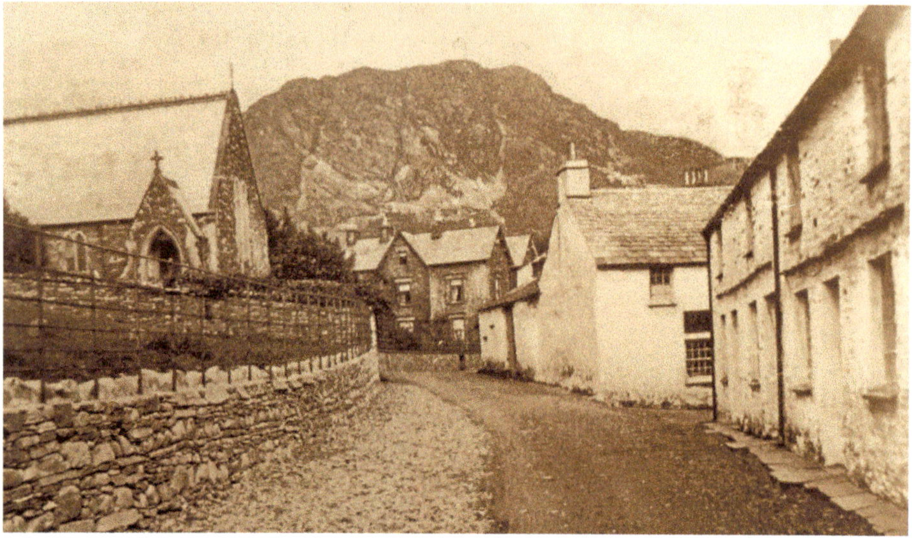

Low Houses, Coniston

The description Low Houses refers to both the single dwelling 'Low House', which faces the road, and the row of cottages running alongside. Low Houses has a long history dating back to the sixteenth century. The white, long house dwelling provided a home for many generations of local families. The smaller cottages housed farm labourers and other workers but were demolished in favour of newer, larger dwellings with a small garden at the front, setting them back from the now busy road. The main house is typically in the Lakeland style, built with dry stone construction and roughcast with walls 2 feet 6 inches thick. Many of its original features have been retained, including an oak staircase and floors. It is mentioned in Sir Daniel Fleming's book of tenants and it has passed through many hands – Tyson, Fleming, Mason and later Wilkinson to name but a few. There was originally agricultural land attached. The house has undergone numerous changes over the years, including partitions and modernisation of rooms. It was latterly acquired by the Midland Association of Mountaineers and provides hut accommodation for climbers and ramblers. From outside it still retains its authenticity.

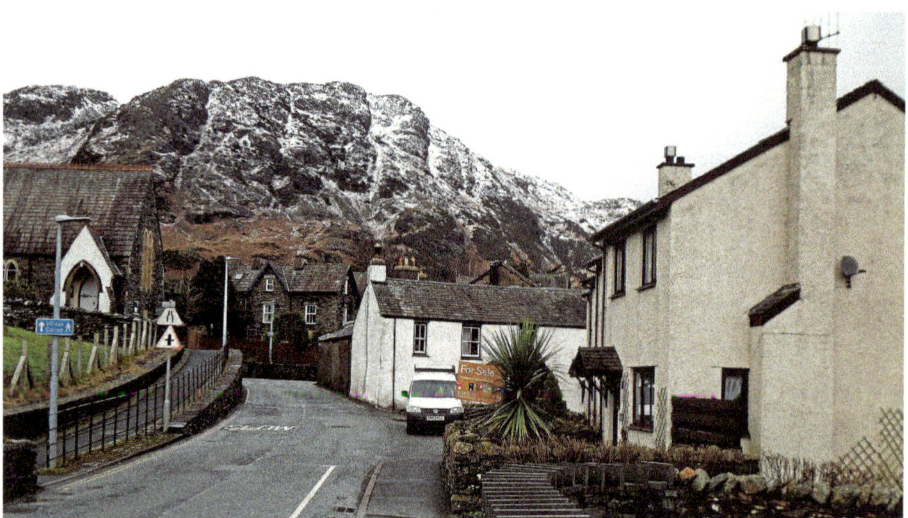

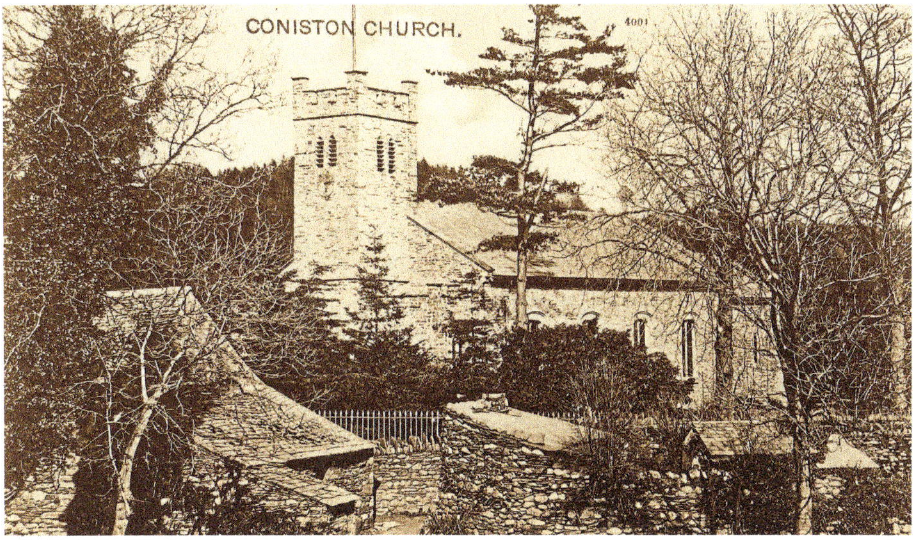

St Andrew's Church, Coniston

There has been a church here from the twelfth century, land at Coniston being divided by William Taillbois, Baron of Lancaster and Kendal, and to the east of the lake the abbot of Furness. The Le Flemings probably built a chapel in the thirteenth century when they became Lords of the Manor. The chapel of ease was probably administered by the Augustinian monks of Conishead Priory near Ulverston. An Elizabethan chapel was built in 1586 and continued to be used until the nineteenth century. The old chapel was rebuilt in 1818–19 and this Georgian church reflected the social hierarchy with the pews and seats. It seems strange to us today, but property owners paid for box pews near the front while the commoners had free pews further back. The years from the 1870s marked a new prosperity derived from influential patrons such as Ruskin, the Severns, the Marshalls of Monk Coniston, and others. Restoration and modernisation was undertaken in 1891 and pews removed. The church looks relatively unchanged today, with hints and features from its rich past. The churchyard is the resting place of Ruskin and a memorial to the fallen of the First World War stands in front of the south porch.

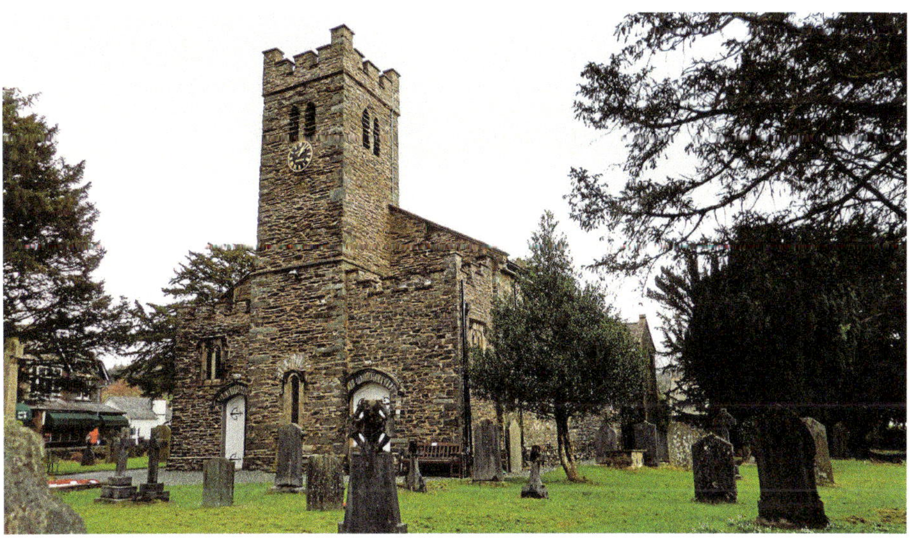

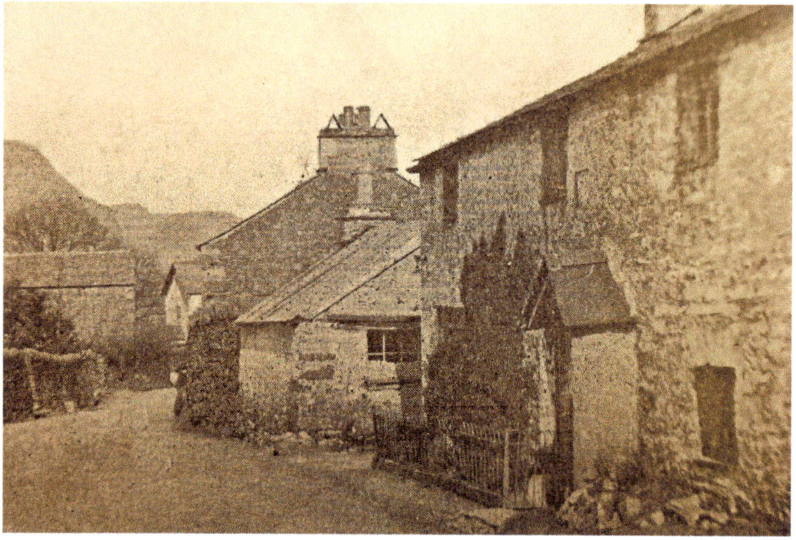

Lake View, Coniston

These old cottages were demolished to make way for housing for the elderly. The bungalows are set further back from the road than the cottages, probably in response to the heavier traffic nowadays. The cottages were small homes and one was once occupied by John W. Knipe, a tailor and draper. The widow of Miles Wilkinson, the gardener at Brantwood, lived here in her latter years. There have been a few changes to property along this busy road and the traditional cottages with their gardens at the back have often been swept away to provide larger accommodation and of course room for cars. This is a sad but inevitable change, with planners and builders responding to the modern needs and expectations of the people they are providing housing for. These small bungalows, which replaced Lake View, are important affordable housing for local people and there are a few other small developments which in the past provided modern and reasonable homes for the indigenous villagers.

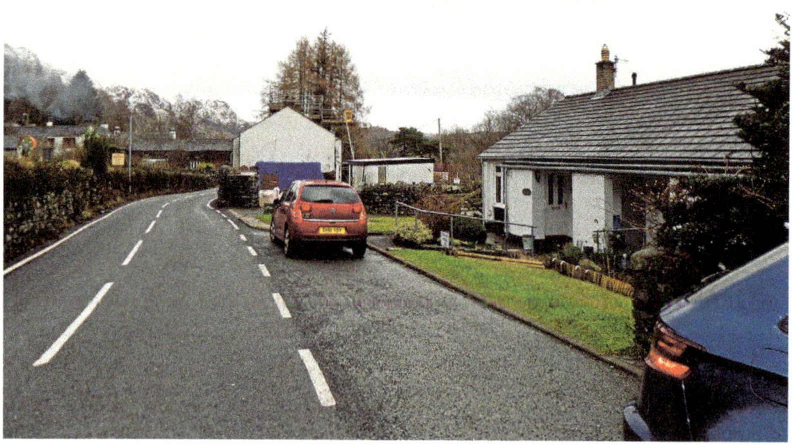

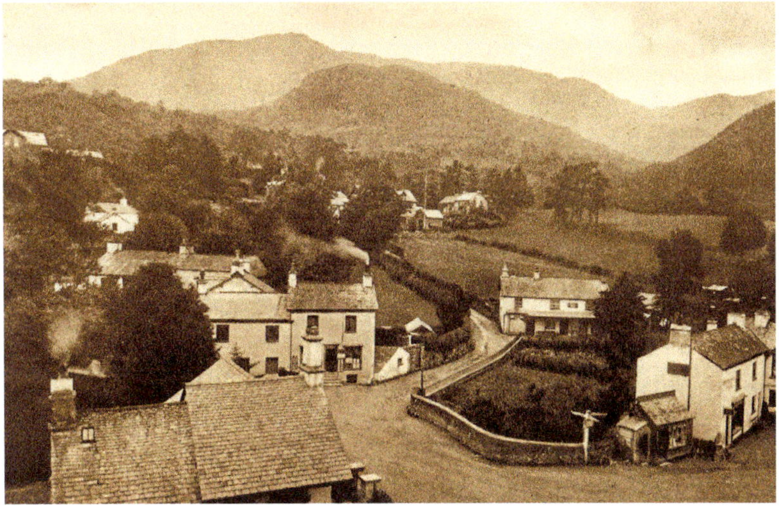

Coniston Village

Settlements in the Coniston area have been recorded from the Bronze Age. Thurston Water, as it was once called, was derived from the Norse name Thorstein and the Old English name *waeter.* This name was used until the eighteenth century and is recalled in the novel by W. G. Collingwood *Thorstein of the Mere.* The Norse settled in the valley and there has been archaeological evidence of this. Coniston is also of Norse derivation and comes from *cyninges tun* or *koenigs ton,* the king's town. The village was important for farming and mining and the various factions in the Middle Ages jockeyed for supremacy over this rich land. The industry developed, and copper mining and slate quarrying have been important to the area for centuries. Tourism and outdoor pursuits have replaced these now, but they are still remembered. Of course, Coniston attracted literary, artistic and creative individuals, not least being John Ruskin, the adopted son of Coniston. The village continues to develop and change, and it constantly provides inspiration for people as diverse as Donald Campbell and his speed trials or Arthur Ransome who captured it in his charming stories in the *Swallows and Amazons* series. The earlier picture is taken from the church tower.

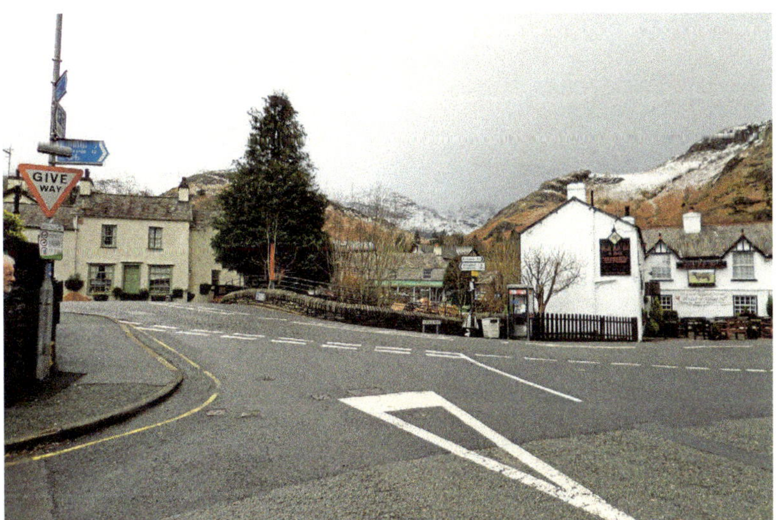

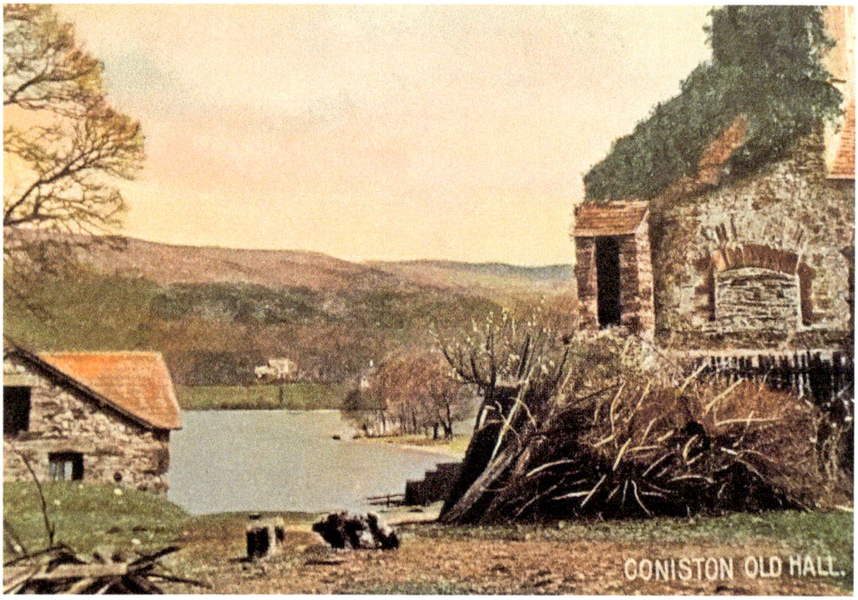

Coniston Old Hall

There is no clear trace of the Old Hall now as the farm buildings have been changed and developed so much. The Old Hall was the precursor to the Coniston Hall we see today, stretching back to the medieval building which was the seat of the Le Flemings, Lords of the Manor of Coniston, who acquired land after disputes with the monks of Furness Abbey, who administered the 'Monk' Coniston lands. This first hall was built by Richard Le Fleming, of which no trace exists today. In the card one can see farm buildings and ruins; it is possible that older remnants lie within or beneath these. The building was begun in 1420 and added to in the following centuries. By the sixteenth century the buildings had degenerated, the Lord of the Manor moving out and a tenant farmer living there. The building was improved in 1815 and this is when the traces of the earliest manor disappeared.

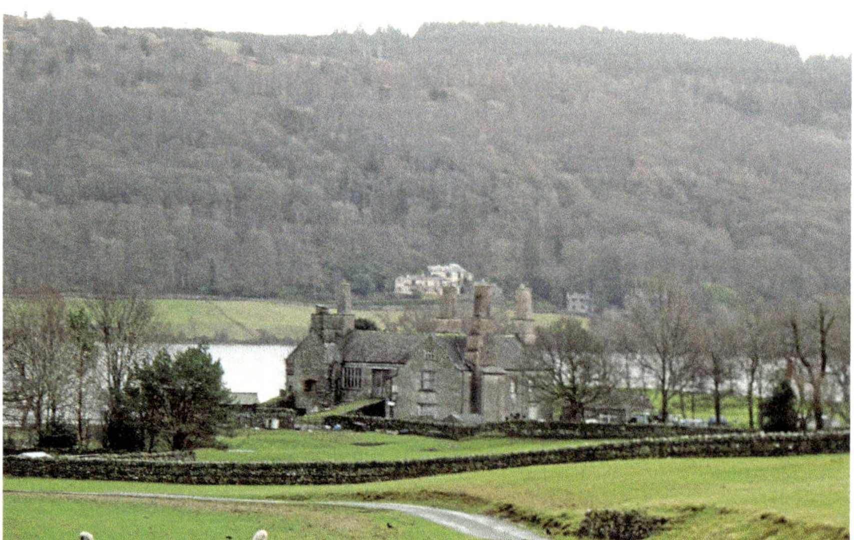

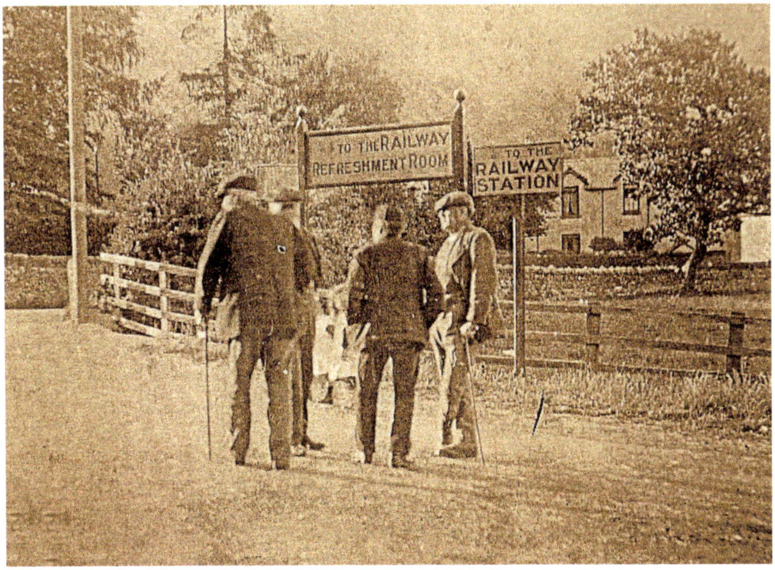

Lake Road, Coniston

The group of men standing in the middle of the road are all local villagers. Back to the camera is John Wilkinson (author's great-grandfather) with walking stick, Ted Gibson, Neddie Swainson and William Dawson Inman (of Coniston Hall). John and Neddie lived until their late eighties and were friends. These family names are still common locally and the prevalent strong community spirit meant that everyone knew each other and provided support for one another. The signage at the junction demonstrates the importance of the railway at that time to the village. The picture was taken around the turn of the twentieth century. The road leads up to the station and is crossed by the main road into Coniston. Lake Road in the opposite direction takes you – as you can guess – to the lake, where the Bluebird Café and tourist car parks now sit. This was the place where the *Gondola* ran from, and excursions took visitors along Coniston Water and back. This fell into abeyance but had now been re-established for the modern tourist.

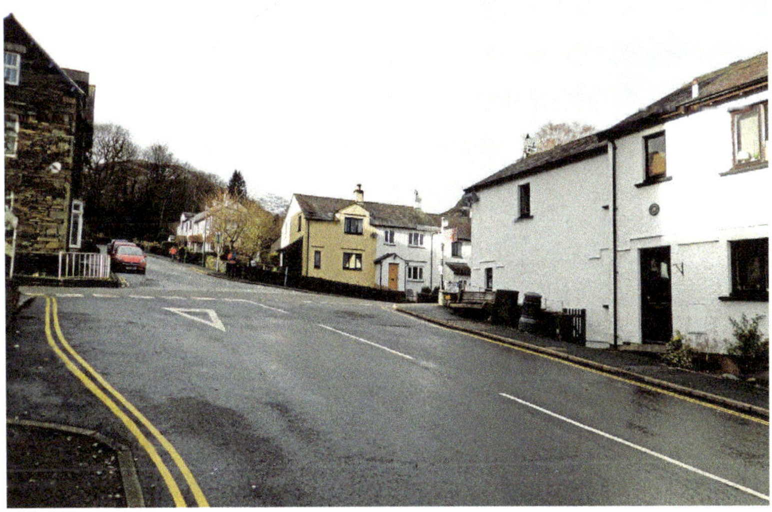

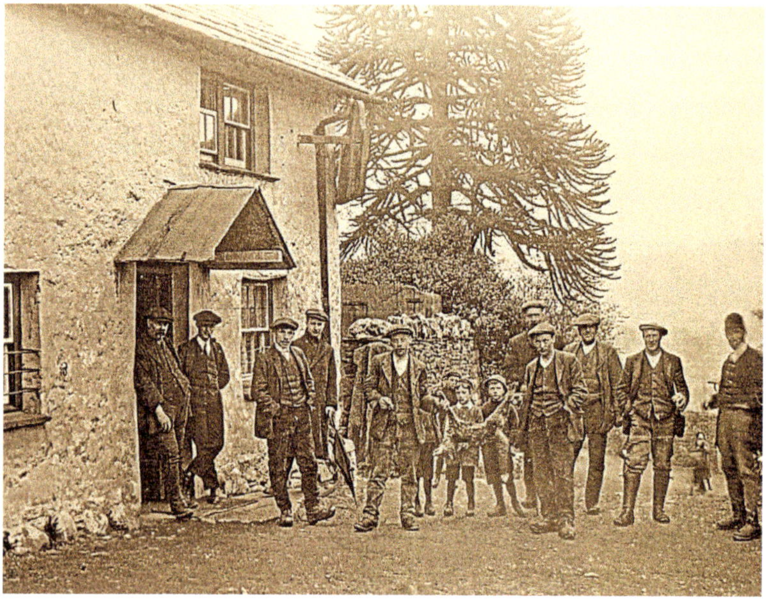

Ship Inn, Coniston

This inn is situated above the lake at Bowmanstead. It retains its old-world charm and apart from the cars parked outside it has changed very little. The photograph shows locals outside the pub after a fox hunt. Hunting was a popular Lakeland sport and was often done on foot and involved all ranks within the community. It was a traditional activity that had been carried on generation after generation; it did not have the same moral objections that occur today. The men left to right are Buttons Barrow, Walter Cheeseman, Billy Mossop, Albert Coward, Tommy Robinson, Billy Proctor. Slightly behind we have Harold Stockdale, W. D. Inman of Coniston Hall, John Thwaites and finally huntsman George Chapman. The children are unnamed but will be local village boys maybe related to the men. The pub is on the main road and is easily passed by, but it is worth a visit. (Picture courtesy of Margaret Thwaites)

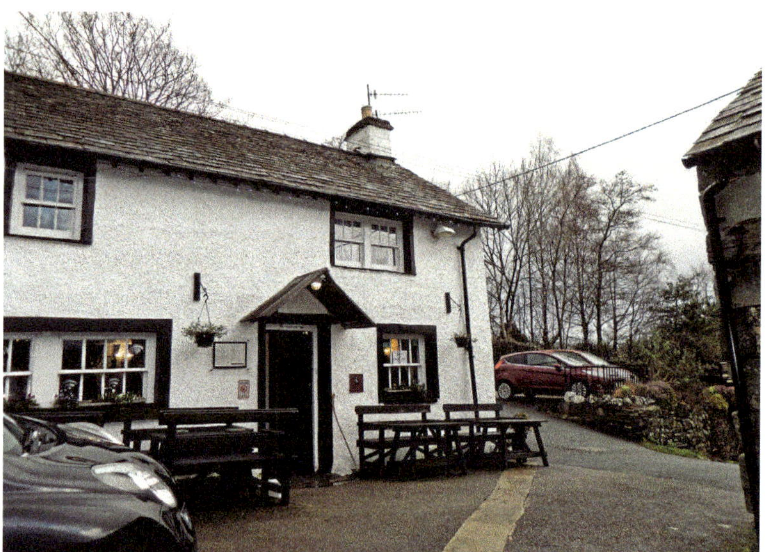

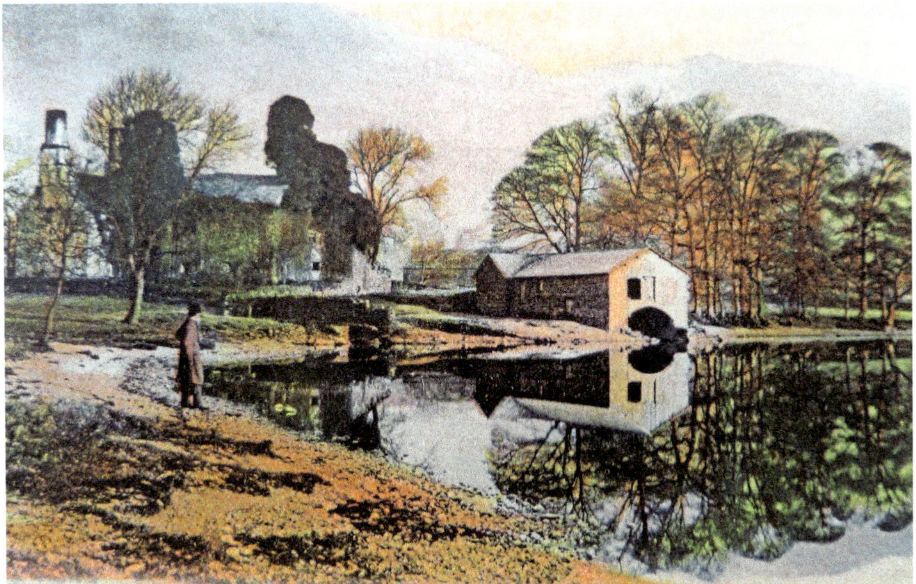

Coniston Hall and Old Man, with the Lake. Abraham's Series

Coniston Hall

The current building stands on the site of the Old Hall and was improved and adapted in the early 1800s. The National Trust bought the hall in 1971 and still administer it today. A caravan and campsite has grown around it and the previous parkland belonging to the Lords of the Manor are used for tourism purposes. Coniston Hall Barn is visible from the road down to the farm and campsite. This was built in 1688 and remained unaltered for many years. In 1974 it was converted by the Trust for the wintering of cows, under great protest by some locals, because of its age. Unfortunately, there was no requirement then for archaeological survey before the building was developed and it is believed that a lot of important evidence was destroyed.

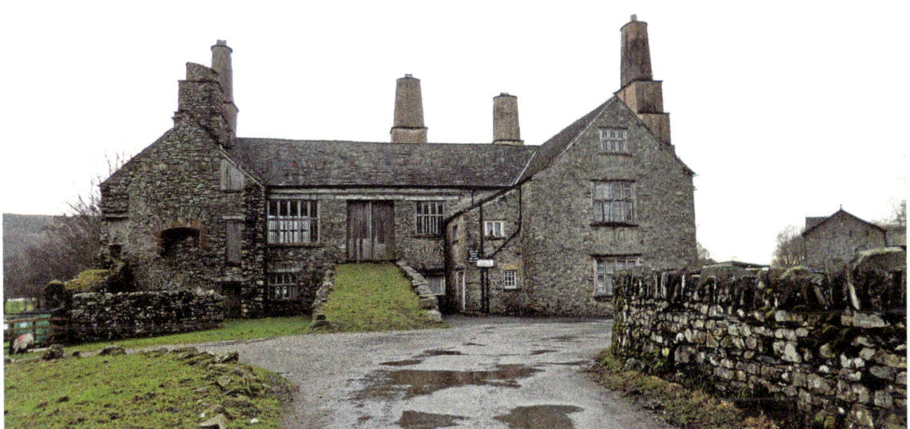

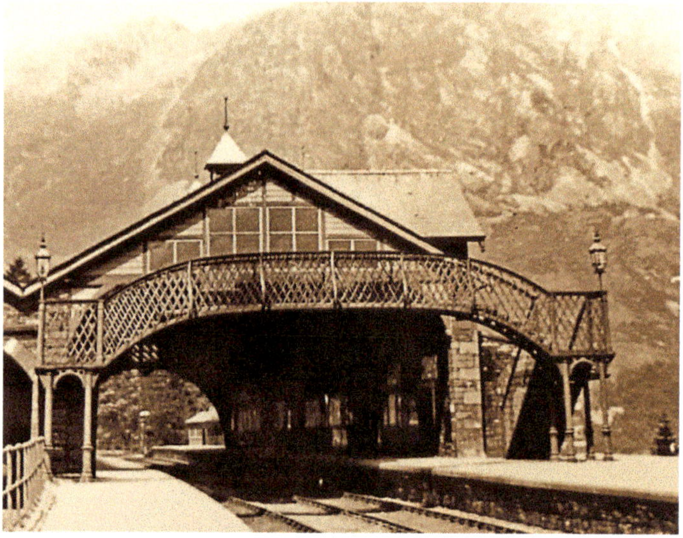

Coniston Railway Station

Coniston Railway opened in 1859 and was used to transport copper ore from the Coniston Copper Mines and connected with the wharf, placed high on the hillside. As well as having a commercial use, the station also brought in tourists to the area. It was designed by E. G. Paley of Lancaster. The Coniston Railway amalgamated with the Furness Railway and the line soon expanded. Furness Railway had two steamers on the lake, the *Gondola* and *Lady of the Lake*, which drew in tourists, but this is inconveniently far from the station. Eventually, the copper ore dwindled and transportation ended. The passenger service which linked to Broughton, Foxfield and Kirkby-in-Furness continued with sharply falling numbers until closure in 1957 when it was estimated a mere eighteen people travelled daily. The steam boats stopped running and *Lady of the Lake* was scrapped, while *Gondola* was sunk in the lake. In 1958 the station and line were dismantled, and some items were used elsewhere, like the footbridge which was removed to Ravenglass and Eskdale Railway (Li'le Ratty). The site is now commercial but there are information boards describing the previous use.

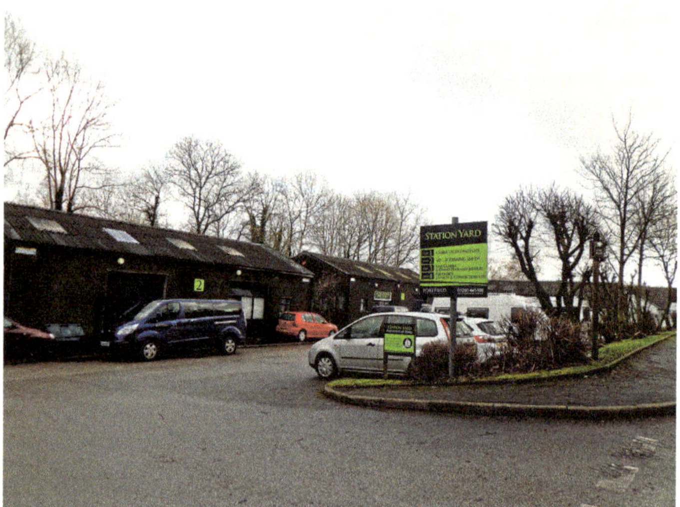

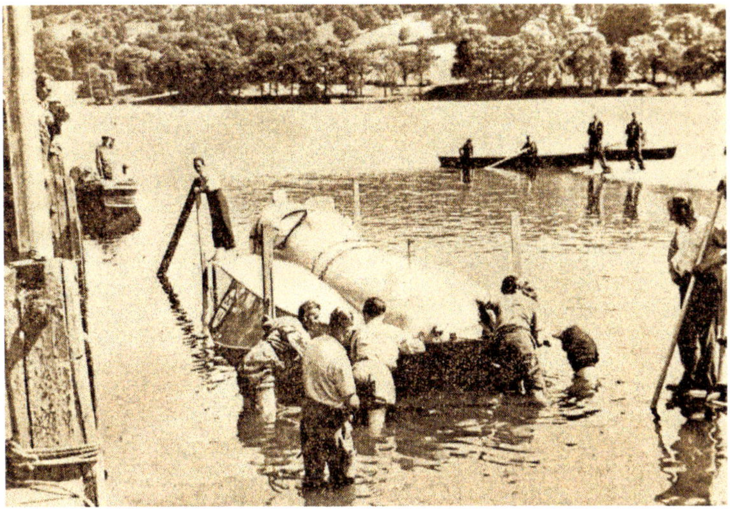

Campbell and Coniston

A café named after the *Bluebird* commemorates the attempts to break the water speed record which Donald Campbell, and before him his father Malcolm, had set. The café was originally built by Furness Railway to accommodate the crew of the SY *Gondola*. It was later frequented by Campbell and his wife Tonia Berne during the speed trials he undertook. The 5-mile-long lake at Coniston was chosen as the best place to hold the trials. On 4 January 1967 *Bluebird K7* was travelling at almost 320 miles per hour when the nose tipped, and Campbell lost control. The boat broke up and sank to the bottom. Campbell remained unfound until 2001 when both he and the wreckage of the *Bluebird* were discovered. He had previously set eight speed records, seven on land and one on water. The photograph of the launch is of an earlier vessel, *Bluebird 11*, which was his father's, Sir Malcolm Campbell's, boat – he failed to break the record on this occasion. His final attempt was fraught with difficulty and issues with the weather. Campbell's funeral was held at St Andrew's in Coniston and he is buried in Coniston cemetery.

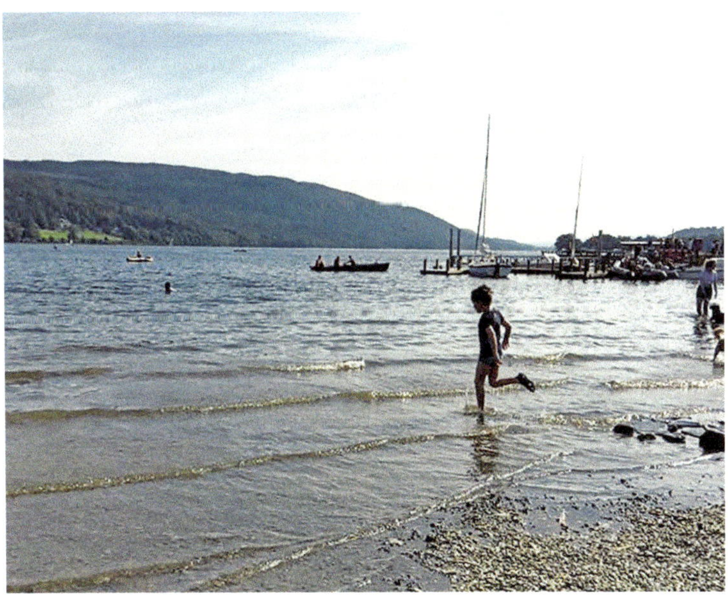

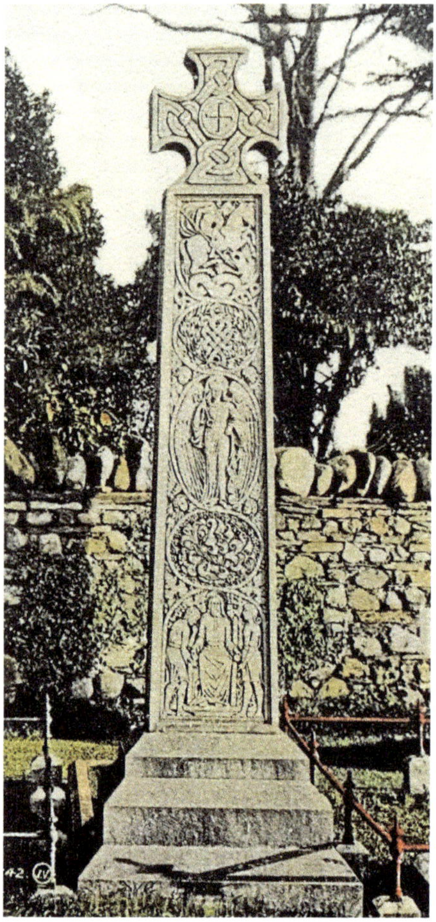

Ruskin's Grave, Coniston

The humble churchyard of St Andrew's in Coniston is the resting place of one of the leading art critics in Victorian England. He was a patron of the arts and a painter and writer in his own right and a social reformer and philanthropist. In his later life he left London and bought Brantwood, where he lived from 1872 until his death in 1900. He had celebrated his eightieth birthday the year before but died of influenza on 20 January 1900. He was buried at his own request in Coniston, where he had been an influential presence for almost thirty years. His grave sits at the back of the churchyard and has an impressive Celtic cross designed by his friend W. G. Collingwood. It is inscribed with signs and symbols that reflect his interest in nature, geology and art. The design maquette is now in the Ruskin Museum, located behind the Village Institute. The day of his funeral was characteristically wet, which Ruskin would have coined as 'pathetic fallacy'. His grave is surrounded by numerous others from the art and literary world including W. G. Collingwood, his son R. G. Collingwood and H. R. Hall RA, a landscape artist who lived in Coniston in the early part of the twentieth century.

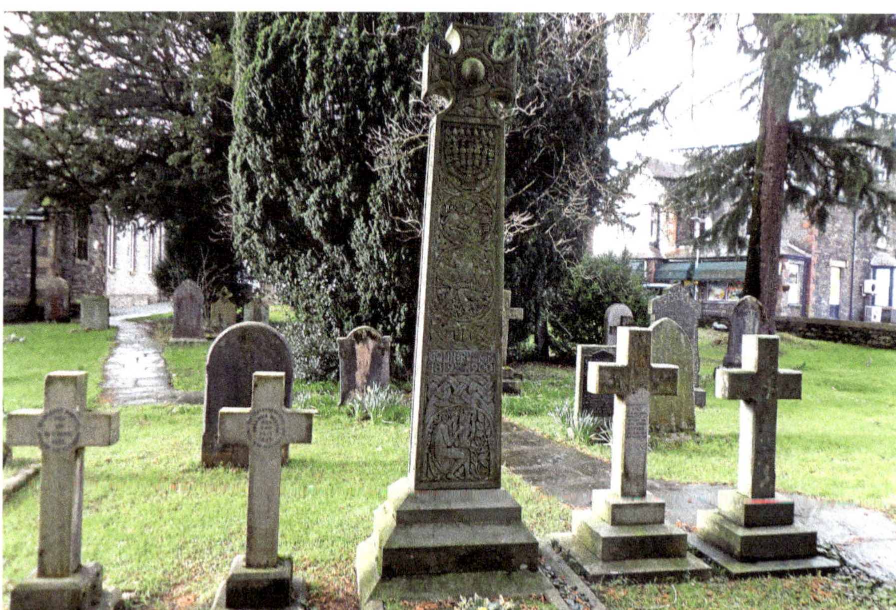

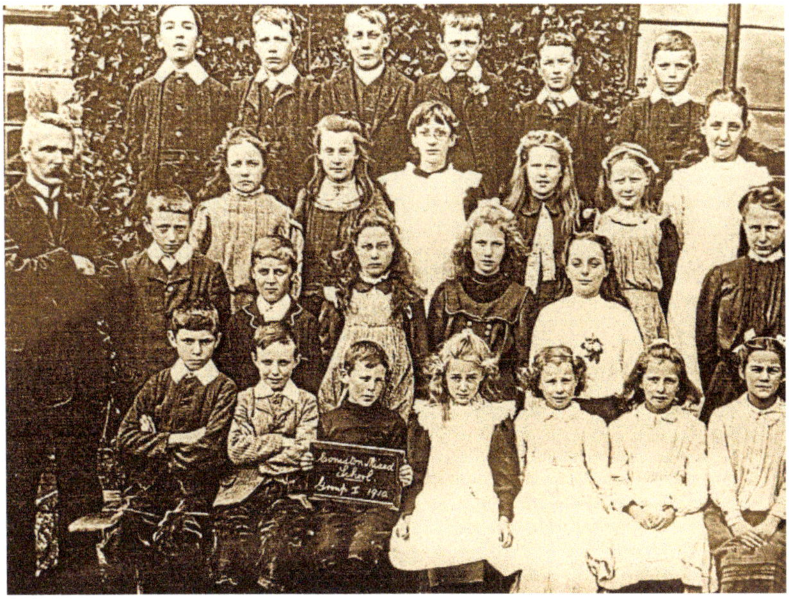

Coniston School

Two new schools have replaced the Victorian schoolroom and are on the outer edge of the village. There is Coniston CE Primary School in Shepherd's Lane and John Ruskin School in Lake Road for older children. The school served many children from the village and the outlying district. The picture is from 1910 and the children are ranked in rows for their annual photograph. The schoolmaster, Mr Rich, looks very severe and from family anecdotes he was a hard task master not averse to the use of corporal punishment. The school was a church school and taught the basics necessary for a good Christian life. As children reached twelve or thirteen they were able to become 'half-timers', whereby they still received an education but were able to work as well. It is a far cry from the experience of today's scholars. The school is now a private house. (Picture courtesy of Margaret Thwaites)

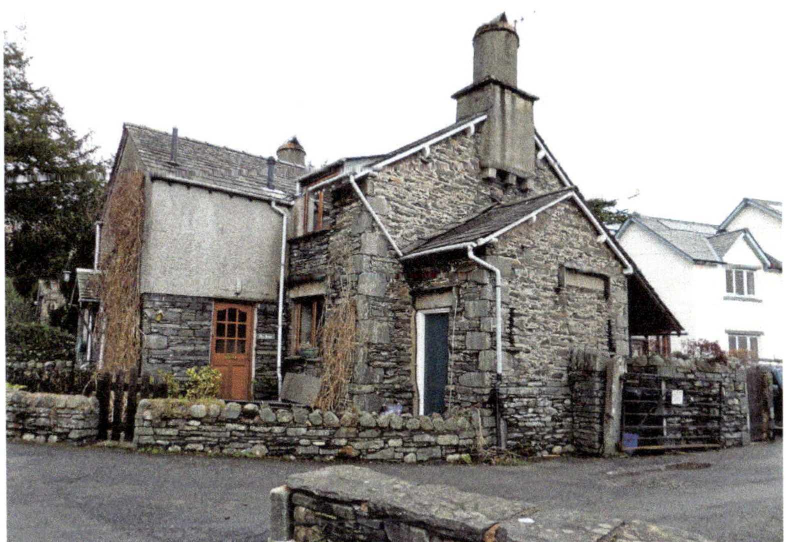

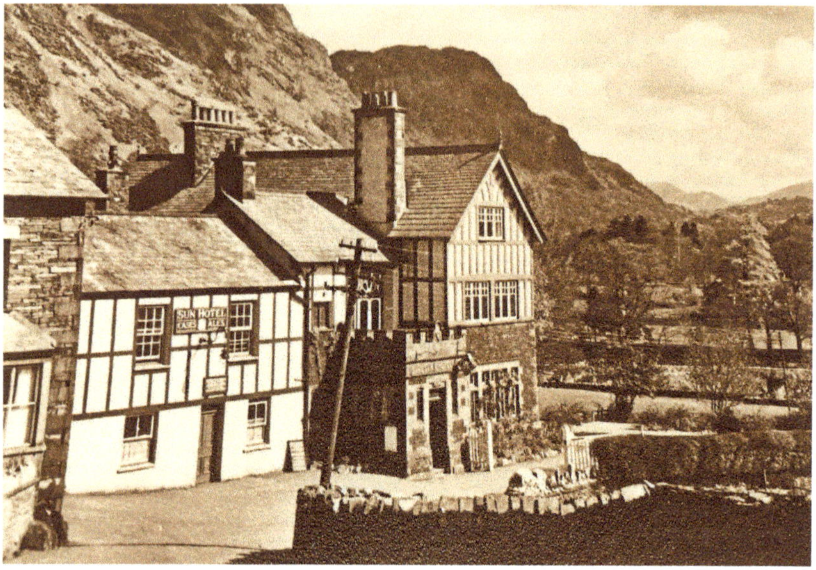

Sun Inn, Coniston

Perched on the hillside above the village, this coaching inn still cuts an impressive image. I warm to the strapline for this hotel on their webpage: 'Not a Travel Lodge – a creaky old building with a great bar, lounge and garden.' It looks almost unchanged from outside and it boasts many original features inside. It was an important inn even before the railway arrived in the nineteenth century and had existed for at least 400 years, being situated on the packhorse route. The hostelry was extended to accommodate the growth in tourism to the area and sits impressively beneath 'Coniston Old Man'. Many of the villagers, including youngsters, were employed there in the early part of the twentieth century. Boys such as Joe Thwaites worked half a day in the morning, cleaning boots, emptying spittoons, cleaning and filling oil lamps – in fact many of the menial tasks in the hotel. When guests arrived in carriages, he tended to the horses and was also responsible for handing out menus to passengers alighting from the bus and steamer and of course the railway. Work being done, he could then return to school in the afternoon.

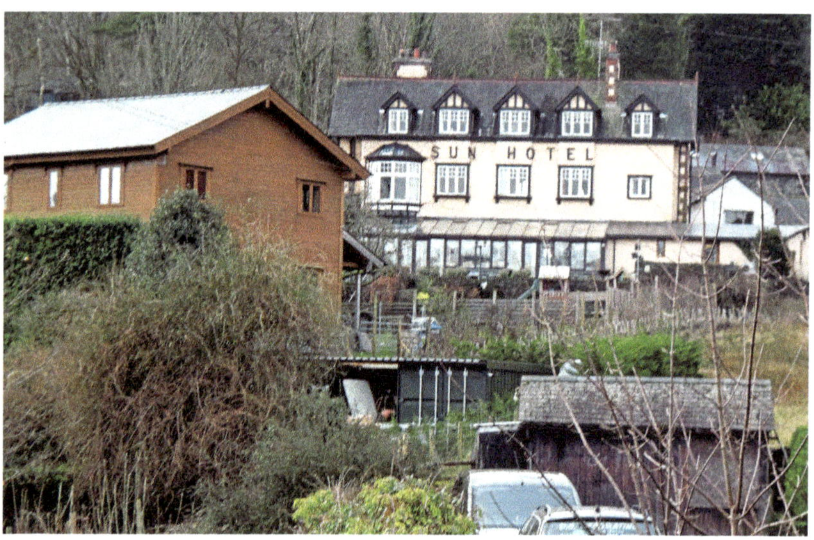

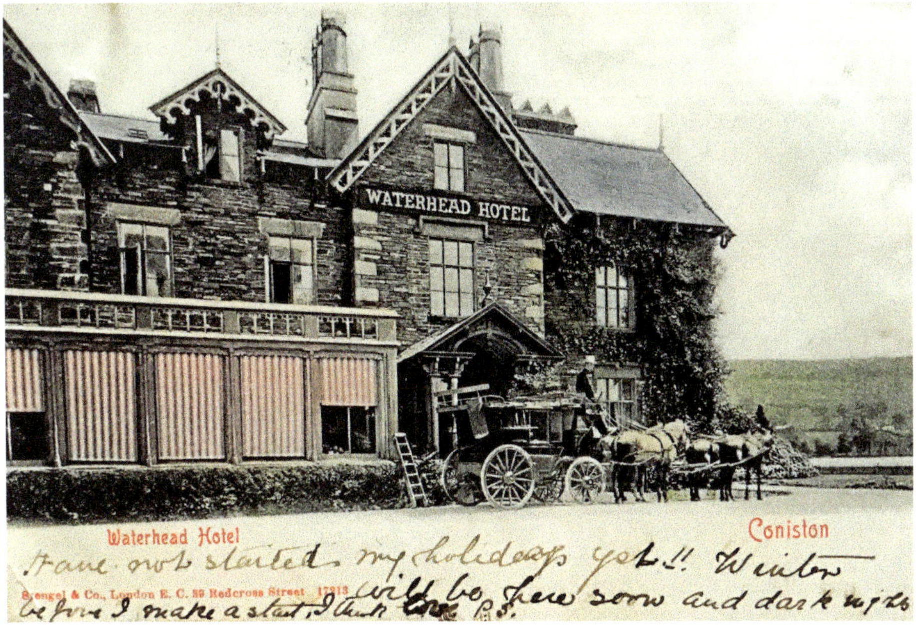

Waterhead Hotel, Coniston

This began life as an alehouse and was popular during the nineteenth century. However, in 1850 the original inn was demolished. The new hotel is a Victorian Gothic building and has splendid views across the lake. The destruction of the old inn was protested strongly by local people and even Ruskin objected fiercely. However, the hotel that replaced it became a popular venue and is still recognisable externally. Many illustrious guests stayed at the hotel, such as Charles Darwin. The hotel was transformed into a school during the Second World War and had Sir Robin Day among its pupils. The first photograph shows a coach and horses waiting for visitors and there is a ladder propped against the wall for people to climb onto the vehicle.

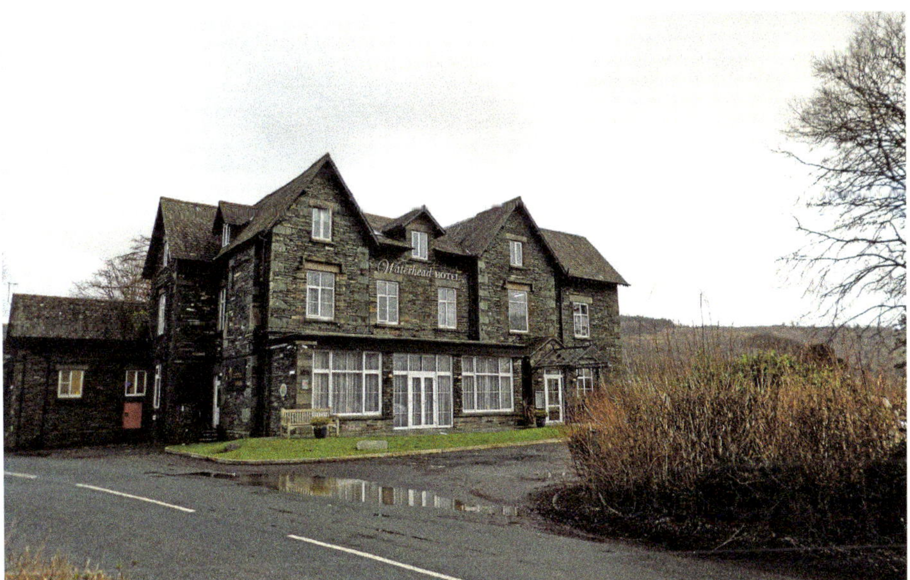

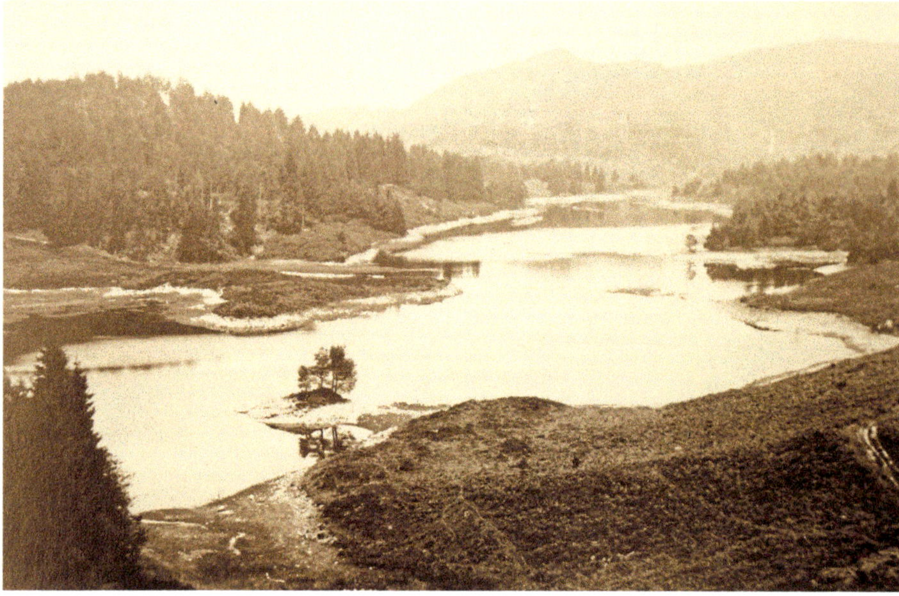

Tarn Hows

The classic view of Tarn Hows has not changed noticeably since it was first created in the nineteenth century. It was made from three smaller tarns which were combined to produce the body of water we see today. The tarns were called – rather uninspiringly – Low, Middle and High Tarn. The tarn flows out into Tom Gill falls onto Glen Mary Bridge (named by Ruskin as more appropriate and romantic than the plain Tom Gill). The outlet beck was dammed to form the tarn in 1862 by James Marshall, the landowner, to form the tarn as we see it today. Trees were planted around the edge of the lake and it is this which gave it the distinctive look it has today. The thick woodland enhances the view and makes picturesque reflections on the water, while the views open to reveal Wetherlam, Helvellyn and the Langdale pikes.

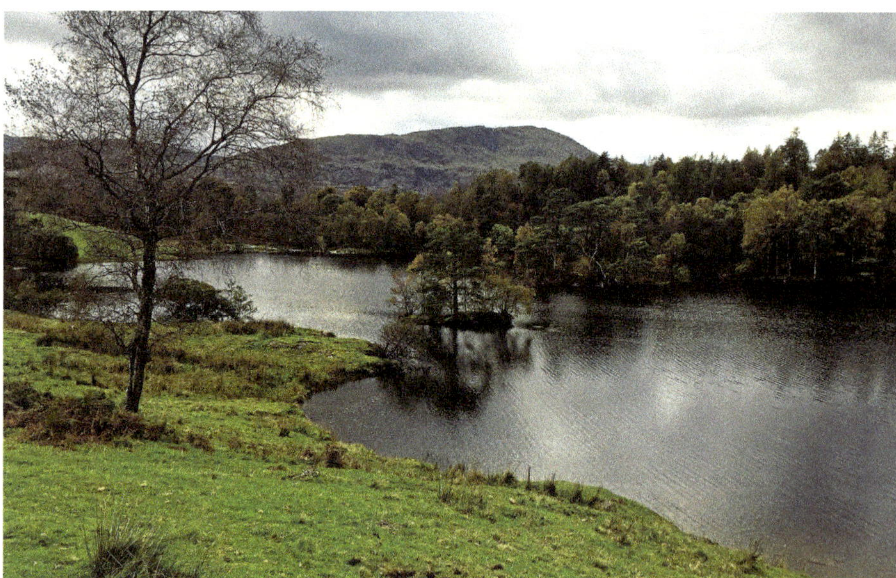

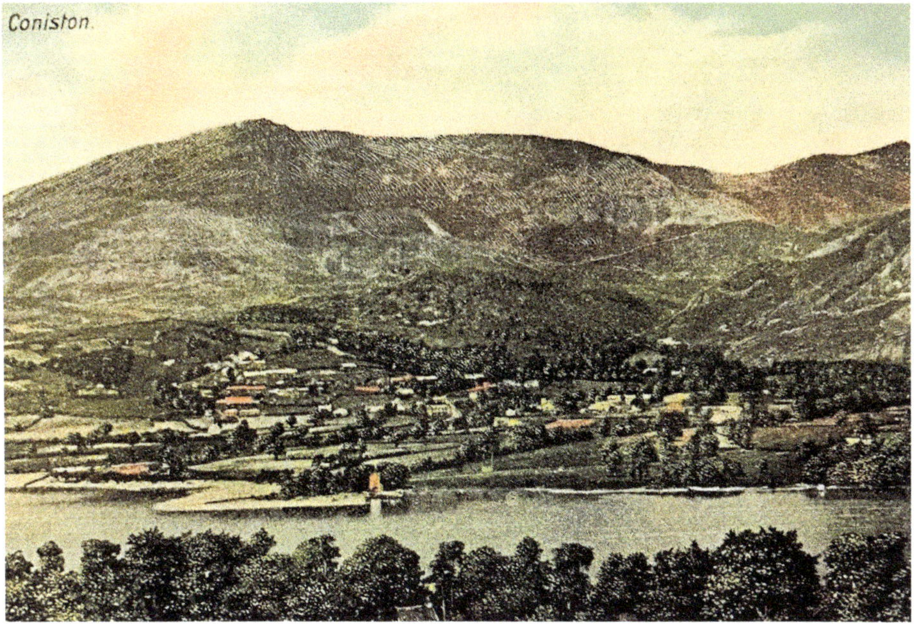

Coniston Water and Coniston Old Man

The view of Coniston Old Man and the village across the lake is very beautiful and it changes in colour and texture according to the weather and light. This is the daily view that Ruskin was lucky enough to enjoy from his home on the east side of the lake at Brantwood. The village is visible in both pictures and Coniston Hall can be seen opposite Brantwood. Coniston Old Man is still a popular place to walk. There are numerous paths up the mountain and it dominates the surrounding scenery. The mountain is 2,634 feet high (803m) and sits within the Furness Fells. The fellside is littered with the remains and spoil tips of the slate mining which has been carried out over centuries. Sheep graze the hillsides, as they have done for hundreds of years, and are a distinctive feature in the unchanging landscape.

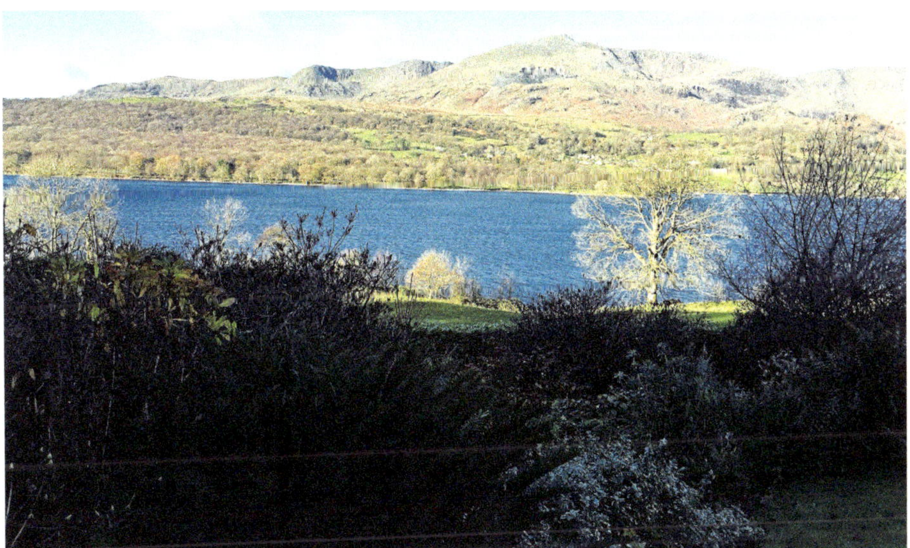

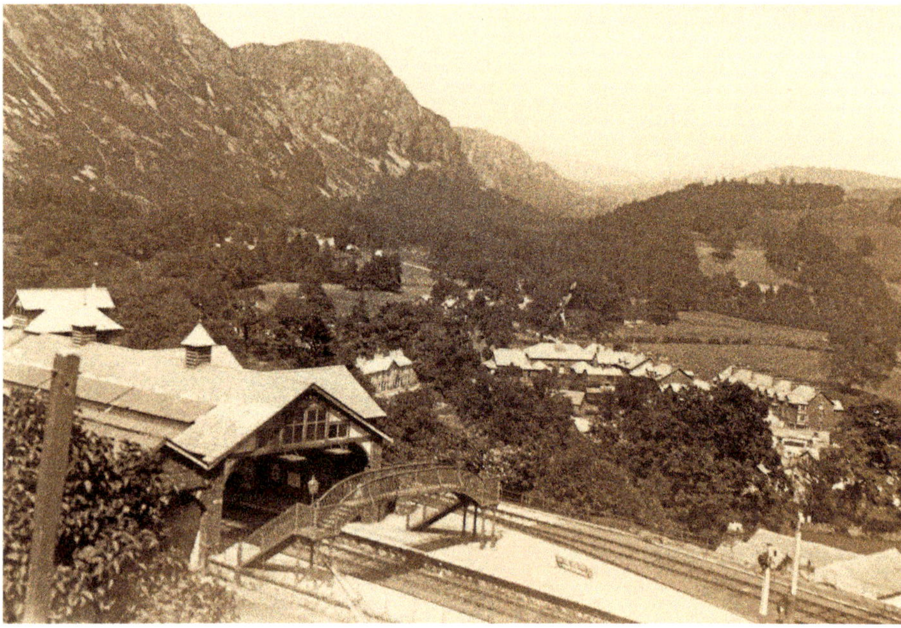

Railway Station and Loading Bay

The loading bay is still evident and sits opposite the station site. This bay was where the copper from the mines was loaded to be shipped out of Coniston. There is now a plaque to commemorate its original use. This area would have been a hive of industry in 1859 and the position of the station arose from the need for rail transport for the copper industry, the passenger service being a later addition. It was a major change for the copper industry and provided a more efficient transport method for removing the ore. The position of the station and loading bay are dictated by the access to the mines, convenient for shipping ore, less so for passengers who faced a good steep walk into the village or to the lakeside.

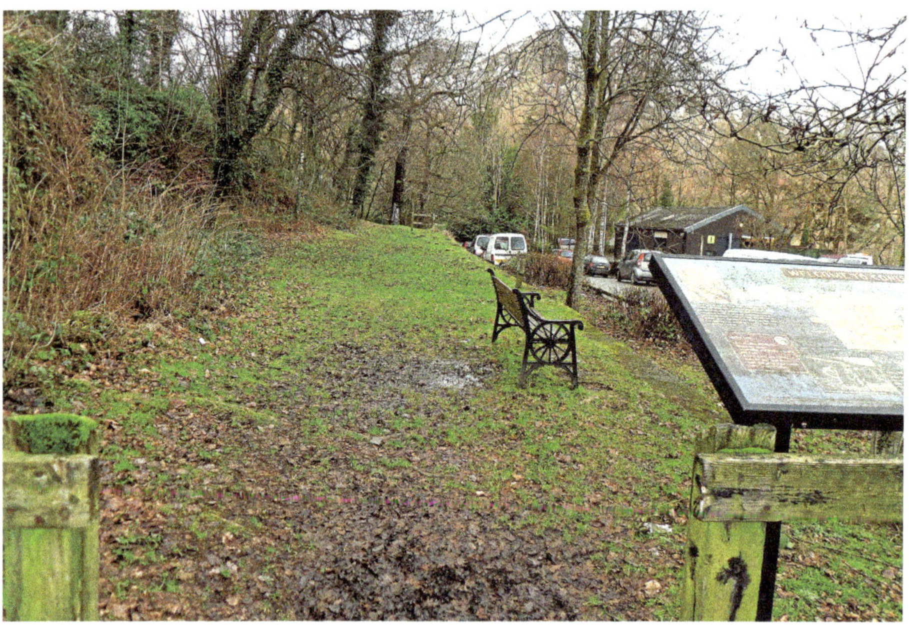

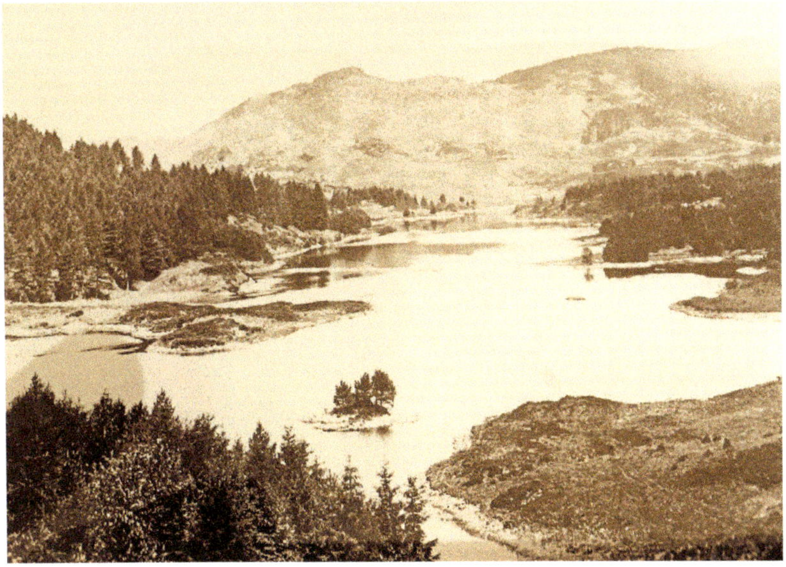

Tarn Hows, Lake Walks

By 1899 the area had become a popular beauty spot and the woods were expanding, spruce, larch and pine saplings creating a denser vegetation. It became a tourist destination of choice both in winter and summer. Skating parties were held in winter and picnics and walks in summer. This heralded the popularity it holds even now. In 1929 Tarn Hows was sold to Beatrix Potter – by then Mrs Heelis, wife of William Heelis – for the huge sum of £15,000. She speculated on buying this land in the hope that some of it could be repaid by public subscription via the National Trust. She did not want to be forced to sell other properties she had saved to buy this one. She in turn sold on the Tarn to the National Trust and bequeathed the remaining land to them in her will. The Heelis's managed the estate and were asked to continue even after the purchase by the Trust. In 1930 it was announced that the Tarn Hows estate had been donated by Sir S. H. Scott in memory of Sir James and Lady Scott. This suggests that he must have bought this part of the estate in response to the appeal. (Picture courtesy of Kris Jepson)

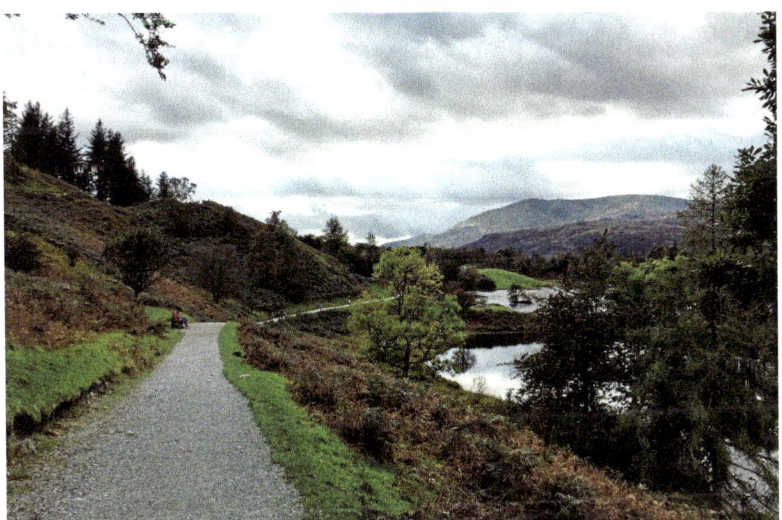

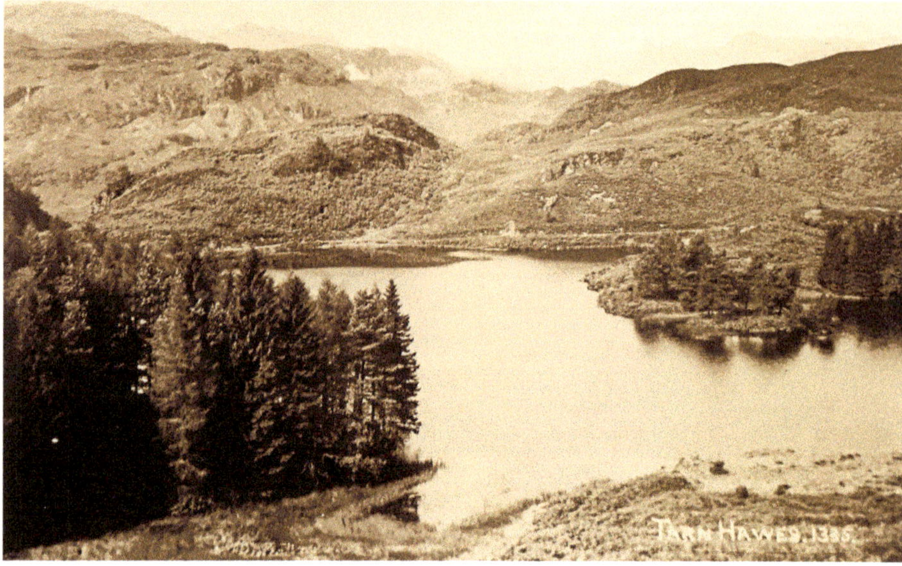

Tarn Hows

Under the National Trust Tarn Hows was designated a place of Special Scientific Interest in 1965. They also manage the car park facilities, which are set back from the beauty spot. There is a constant battle to maintain the paths and walks around the Tarn yet retain its natural beauty. The volume of tourists is ever increasing, and it is as popular as it ever was. Naturally, with growing numbers of visitors the Trust have had to adapt the landscape and provide basic facilities such as toilets and access for disabled visitors. They must blend this with the natural environment and have built an eco-friendly toilet block and information display. Pathways are now accessible for wheelchairs and pushchairs and the walks are graded according to ability. Of course, the purists would suggest that this spoils the natural rigour of the area, but it does at least afford the outdoor experience to all, which provides a positive contrast to our increasingly urban way of life.

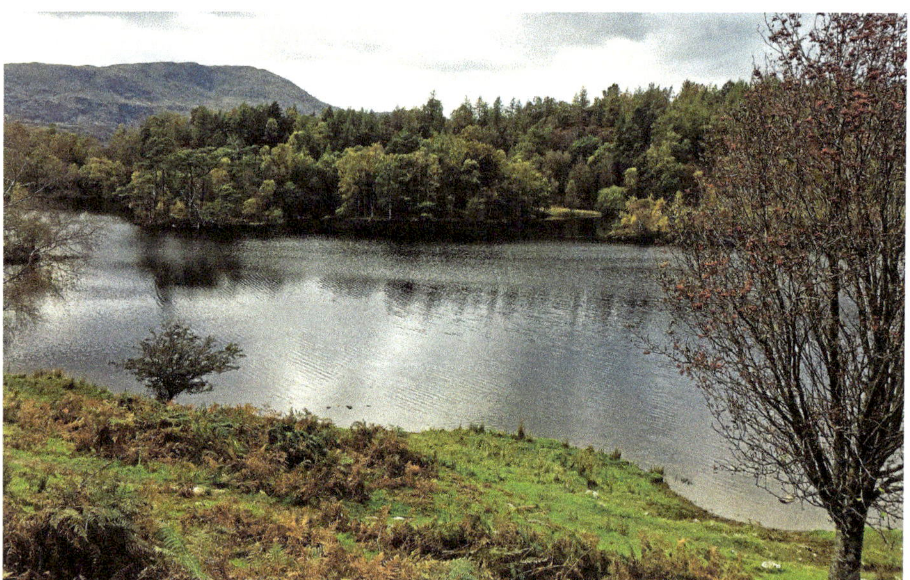

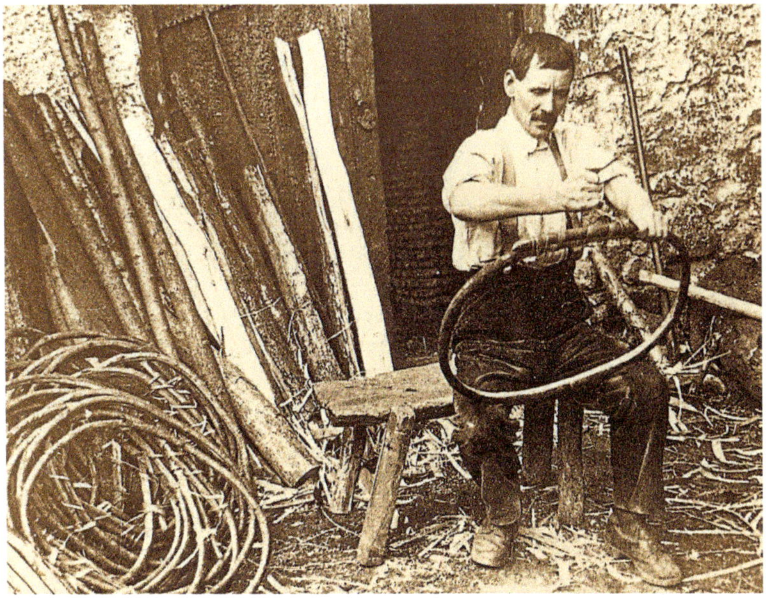

Swill Basket Making

One of the traditional industries in the Lake District was coppicing: the ancient skill of wood management. This produced several other trades including broom and besom making, bobbin making and fencing. The trade shown is that of oak swill basket-maker, which was an allied trade. This trade had not changed for centuries and is extremely skilled work. The need for basket work declined in the twentieth century and so did the trade. The craft was in danger of dying out but luckily there are some people who have devoted themselves to following it. Owen Jones was taught by John Barker, a retired swiller from Broughton, and he has continued the trade and now trains others. He also coppices the wood required to make the baskets. He can often be found at country fairs demonstrating this age-old skill and takes commissions for work.

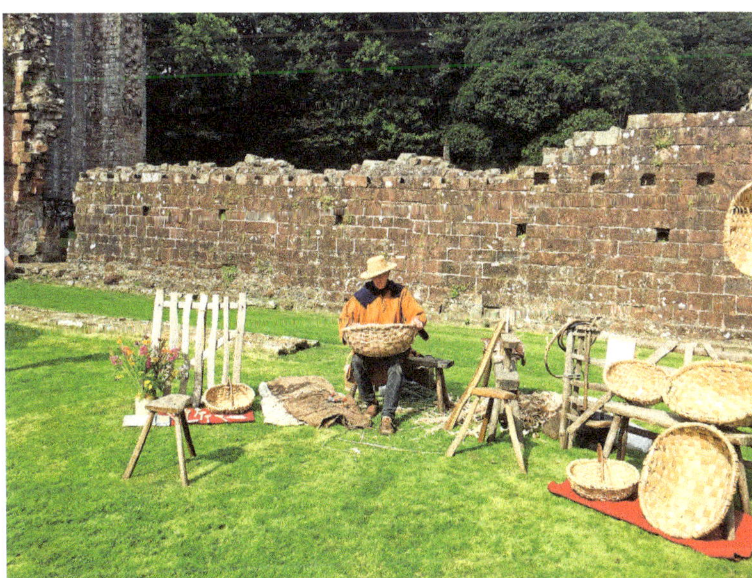

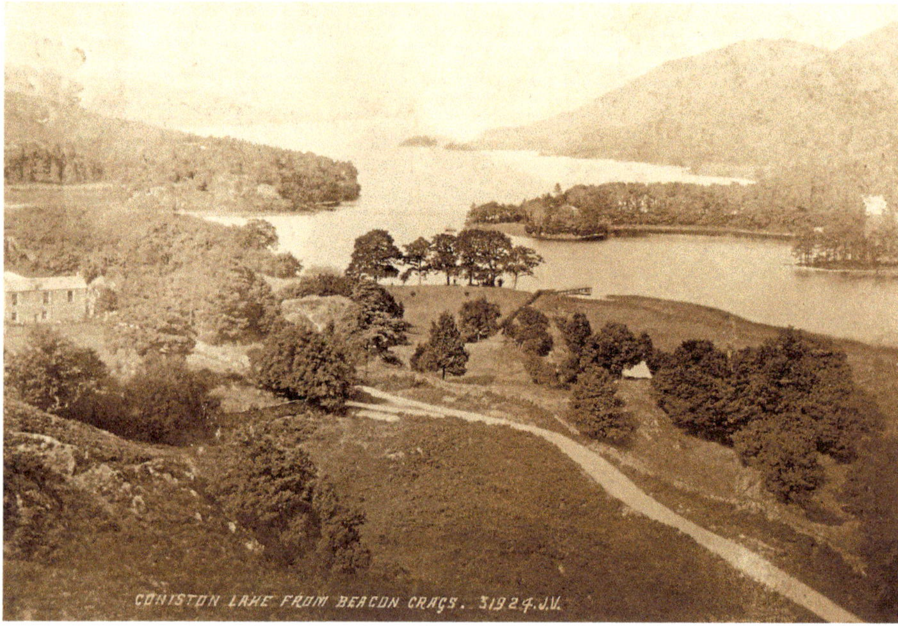

Coniston from the Head of the Lake

This picture of Coniston is from Beacon Crags and gives a clear view up the lake. Beacon Crags is 836 feet (255m) in height and is one of the Wainwrights. It is found in the Blawith Fells and gives a panoramic view of Coniston Water. The rural and agricultural scene, with farmhouses and small islands, is unchanged and the vista shows what man and nature has created over time. The modern view is from the western end of the lake. There are slate walls and boundaries along the edge of the lake with inlets and laybys for the passing motorist to take in the views without the effort of climbing the fellside.

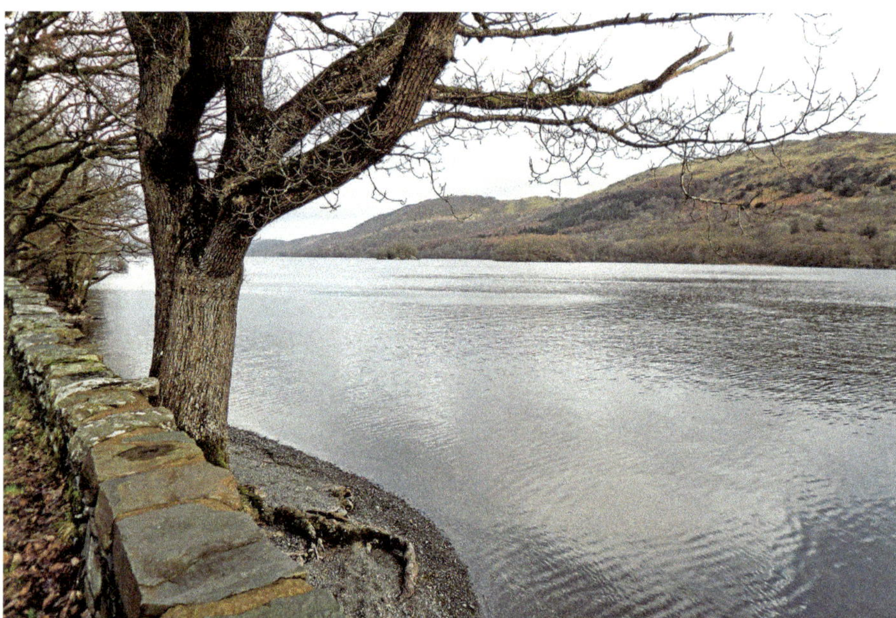

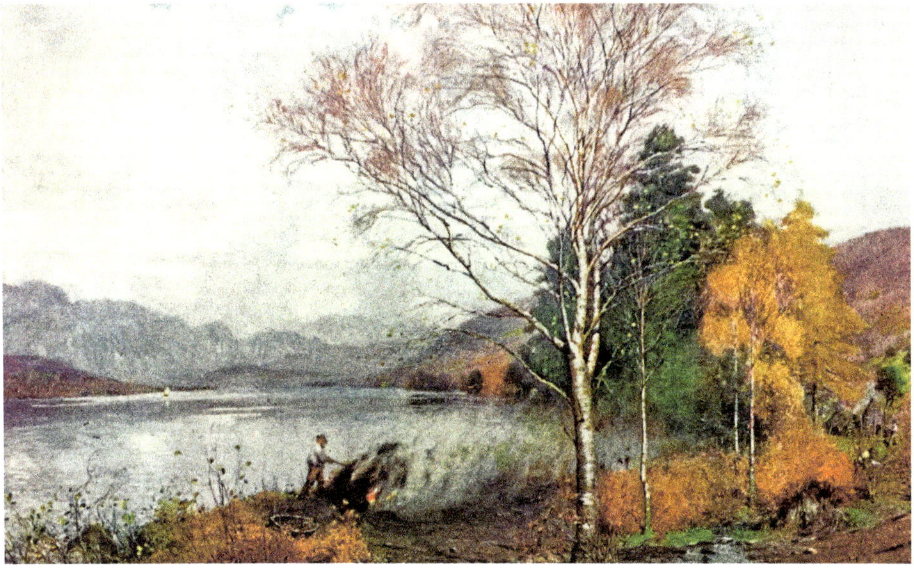

Coniston Charcoal Burners

Woodland trades have always been important in the Coniston area. The banks of the lake are packed with indigenous trees, the colours of which are spectacular in autumn. A blaze of orange, red and burnt browns are as vivid in real life as in the painting. Coppicing is still undertaken locally, and the wood is still sometimes cleared traditionally by horses pulling timber with chains and harness. Charcoal burning was a 'cottage' industry and the men who carried it out could be found in many of the Lakeland woods around Coniston and Windermere. The original painting this postcard was produced from was painted in 1905 by A. Heaton Cooper. The artist painted a series of pictures to be used in the book *The English Lakes*. The images were used on postcards for the public and they capture life in the early twentieth century.

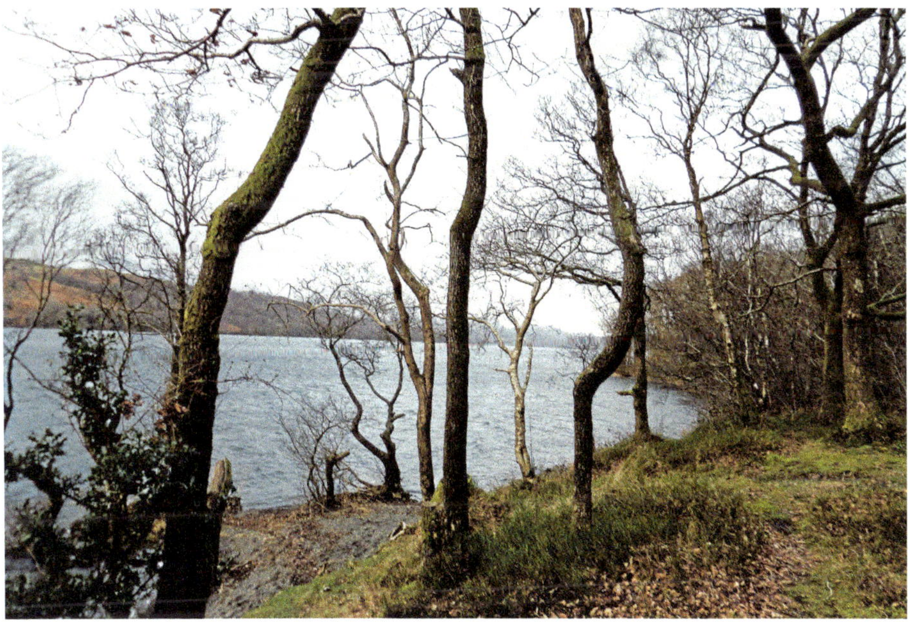

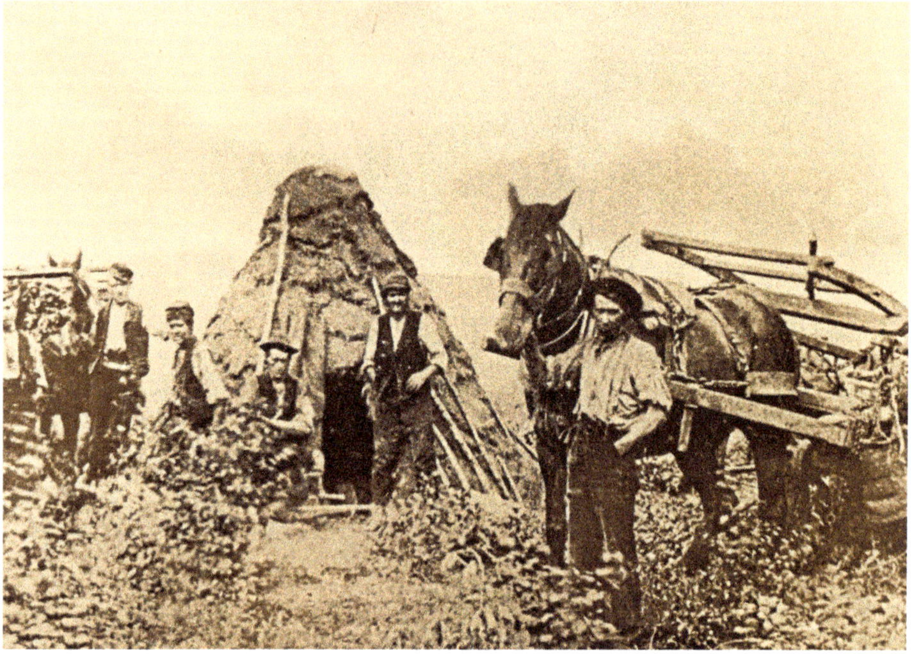

Charcoal Burners

The process of charcoal burning carbonised wood in a pile or kiln. The conical wooden piles were used to make charcoal, and these were burnt over many days; it is an ancient skill and was not an easy job. Originally, charcoal was used in the smelting process and for glass and metalwork. Occasionally, these wood crafts can be witnessed in the area even today; in the summer there is an Earth Burn event annually at Stott Park Bobbin Mill, which is shown in the second photograph. This tradition is practised by only a few specialists, mainly for demonstration purposes. (Photograph courtesy of English Heritage)

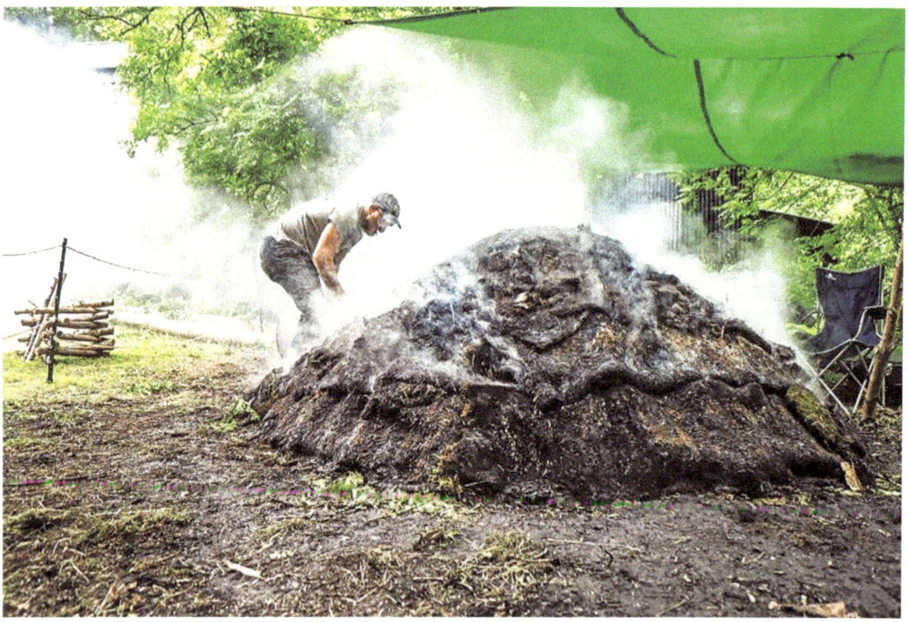

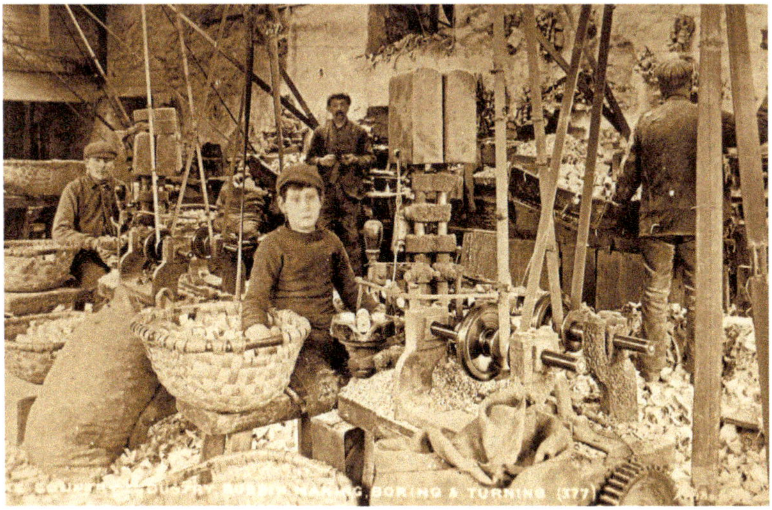

Stott Park Bobbin Mill Interior

This picture is from 1906 and shows the interior of the bobbin mill. The first thing that strikes you is the young boys at the front of the picture. Young boys were frequently employed there, and the work was dusty and dangerous. The working conditions were cold because doors and windows had to be left open to allow the wood dust to dissipate. Often the shavings were allowed to pile up around the workers' legs to keep them warm. Hours were long and conditions harsh, but the mill provided work for those who needed it. It was a successful bobbin mill and was one of the last to close. It still operates, as is evidenced by the workshop in the modern picture. The staff now operates under modern health and safety rules. The steam engine is demonstrated regularly, and people can witness the last working bobbin mill in action. (Photo courtesy of English Heritage)

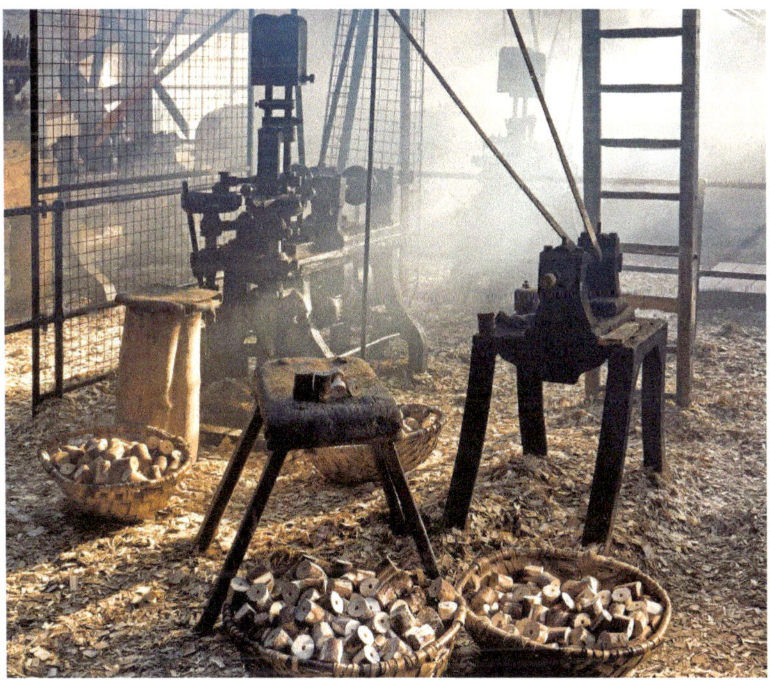

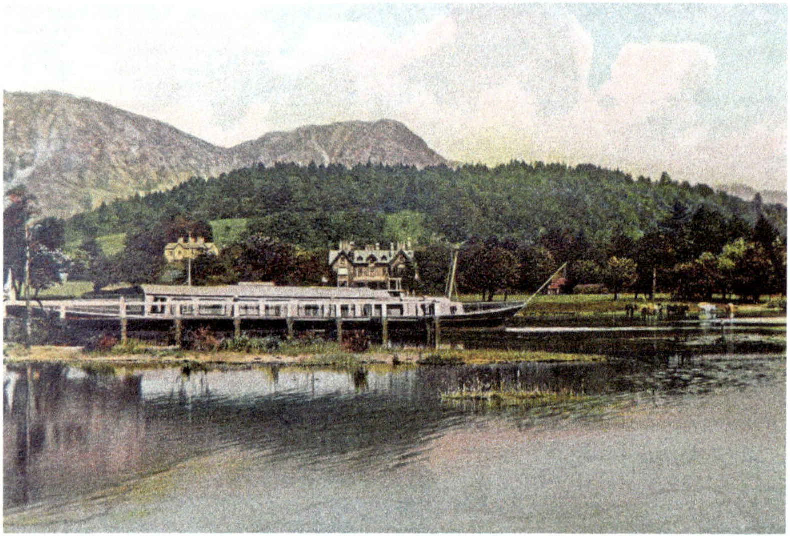

The *Gondola*

The steam yacht *Gondola* was launched in 1859 for the Furness Railway and Coniston Railway for carrying passengers. Sir James Ramsden, director of Furness Railway, was inspired by a visit to Venice and commissioned a steam yacht for Coniston Water from Jones, Quiggin and Co. It was a state-of-the-art screw-propelled, steam-powered vessel which ran until 1936 when it was retired and later turned into a houseboat. Arthur Ransome used the *Gondola* as his stimulus for the pirate Uncle Jim's houseboat in his children's story *Swallows and Amazons*. By the late 1970s it was derelict but was reconstructed and eventually brought back into service. It is a popular tourist attraction once again and is managed by the National Trust. Visitors can take a circular tour from the pier at Coniston to Brantwood, and Monk Coniston. It has around 40,000 passengers annually and is a remarkable story of regeneration.

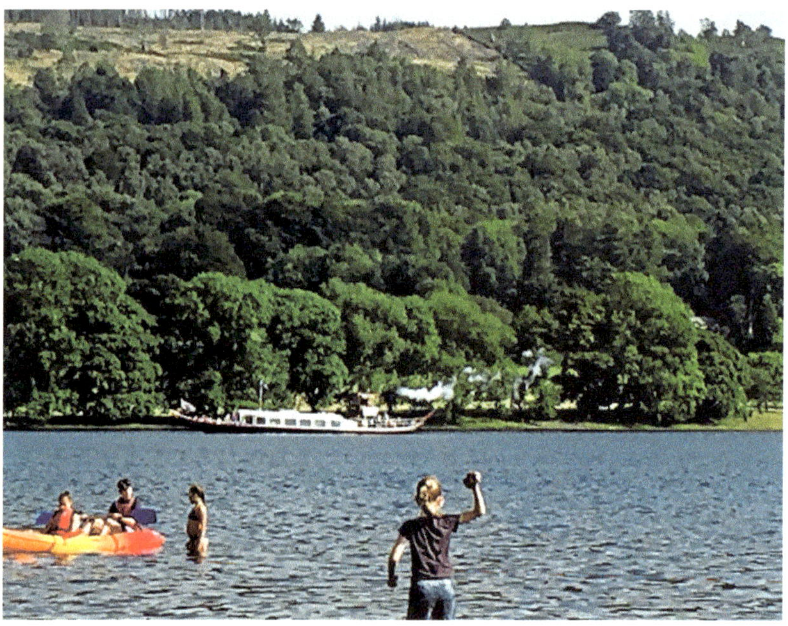

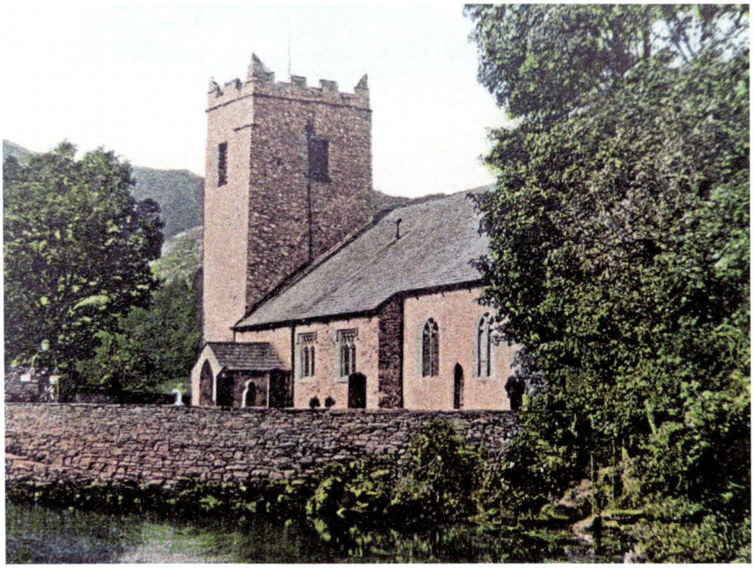

Grasmere Church

St Oswald's Church is situated by the River Rothay in the middle of Grasmere and was originally founded by Oswald of Northumbria in 642. The current church dates from the fourteenth century and was adapted and added to in 1490. The windows and doors were restored by George Webster in 1840. It still retains some medieval features, such as the font and some of the glass in the windows on the south side of the chancel. Naturally, the association with Wordsworth is important and there is a monument to him by Thomas Woolner. The church is famous for the rush-bearing ceremony which happens each year. There are some other interesting features including stained glass by Shrigley and Hunt, an Arts and Crafts font and a statue of the Virgin Mary by Ophelia Gordon Bell. The church has recently undertaken renovation of the tower and the external walls, bringing it back to its former glory.

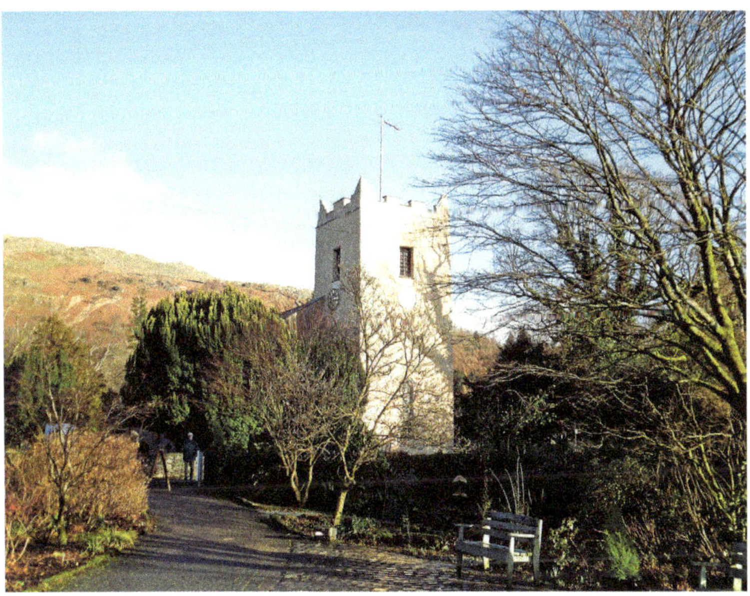

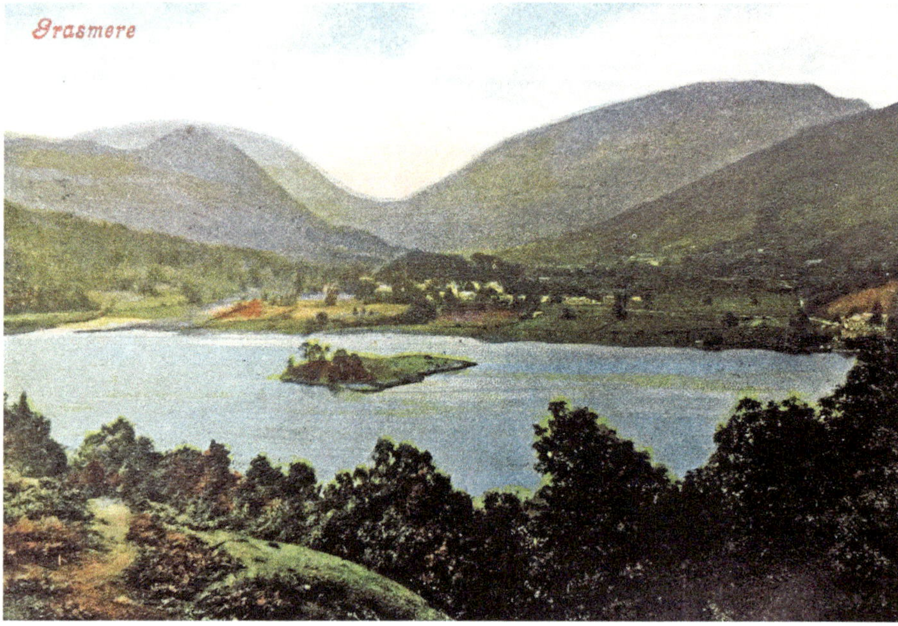

Grasmere from Red Bank

Views from Red Bank up the lake towards the village are amazing. Helm Crag and Dunmail Raise can be seen in the distance and this is a view much painted and photographed and another haunt of Wordsworth. The ascent up Red Bank to Loughrigg where the view is taken from is one of the 'midget mountains' so named by Wainwright. It is a struggle but worth the expansive view from the top. The ancient woods around Red Bank is peppered with paths that meander down towards the lake and around or alternatively up the hill and onto the fell above Elterwater village.

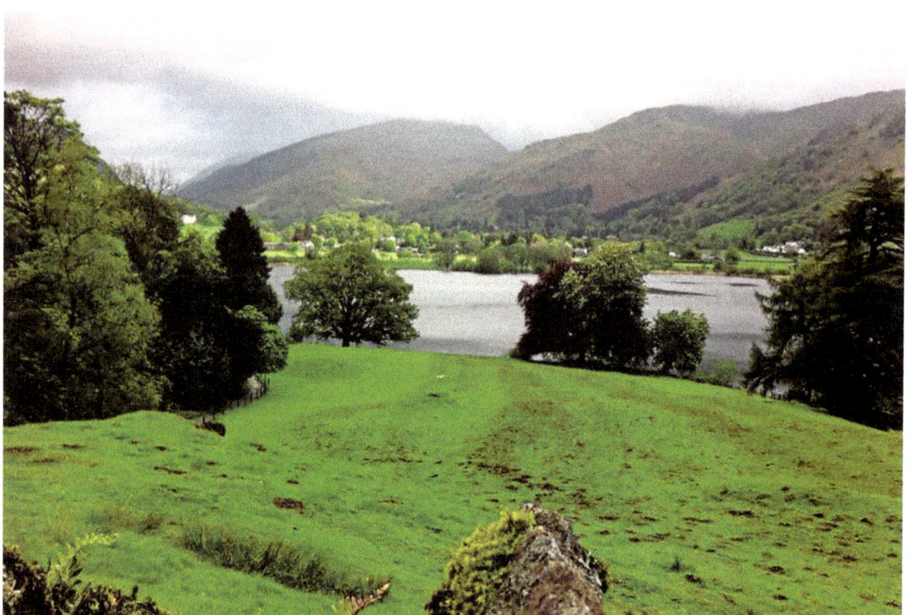

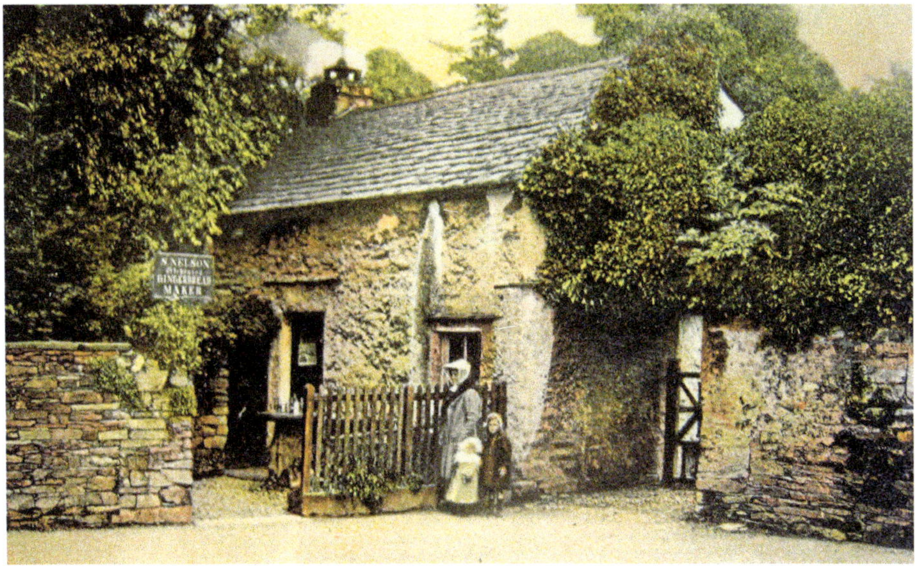

Gingerbread Shop, Grasmere

Grasmere gingerbread is unique and is only genuine if bought from this one shop. The cottage that houses the shop has been sanitised, scrubbed and whitewashed, losing some of its authenticity. The charming period picture is quaint and rural, the sign for Sarah Nelson declaring the sale of this confection. Its popularity does not wane and in the height of summer queues form right around the church with visitors waiting to sample the cake. It has been upgraded now – still quaint but more polished – in the same way many of the other old buildings in the Lakes have been 'improved'. It is beside the lychgate of the church and in the modern view the ivy has been removed and there are numerous signs cluttering the front of the shop. The shop has lost some of its ivy and sports a sparking whitewashed frontage.

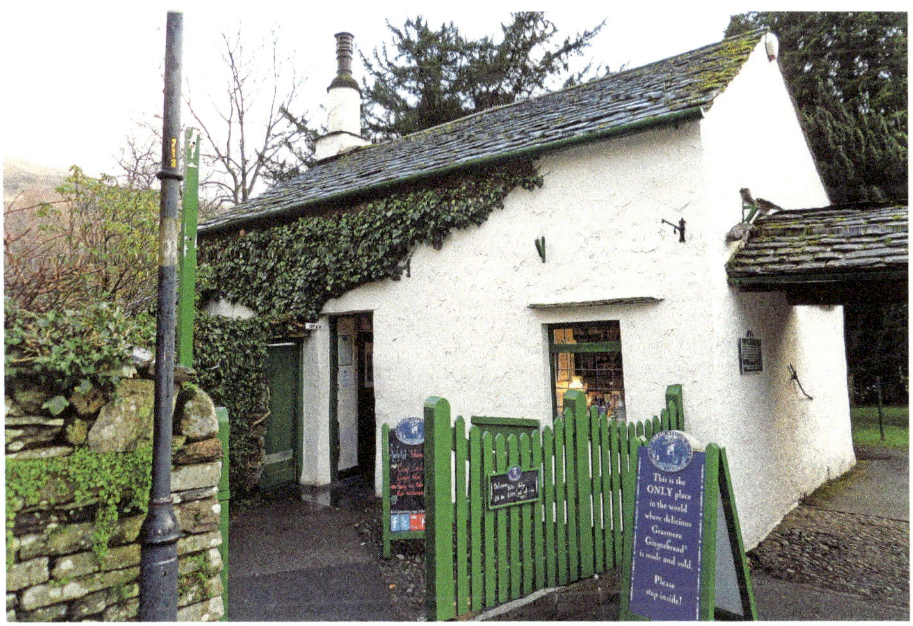

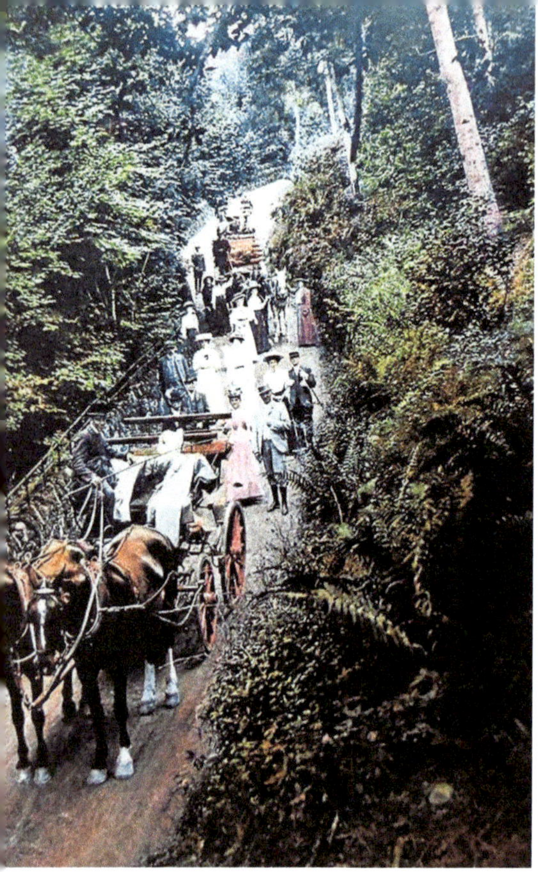

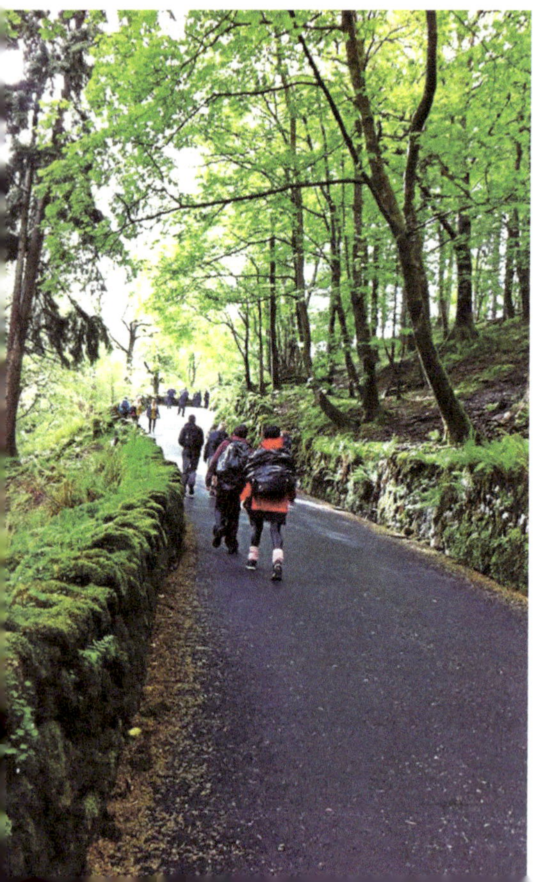

Red Bank, Grasmere

The photograph of the passengers walking down the steep road at Red Bank shows how difficult this fell road can be. The passengers had to walk to prevent the coaches running too fast down this steep incline. It is difficult to walk down but walking up is even harder. It is an integral part of the Keswick to Barrow Walk and produces one of the steepest parts of the course. The incline at one point is 25 per cent and even in a car it is a challenge. It looks innocuous when at the foot, but it very quickly becomes incredibly steep. It is a popular cycle route as well and is very arduous. However, it is a beautiful route up to the top of the fell and the view across to Elterwater and the Langdales at the top is worth the agony.

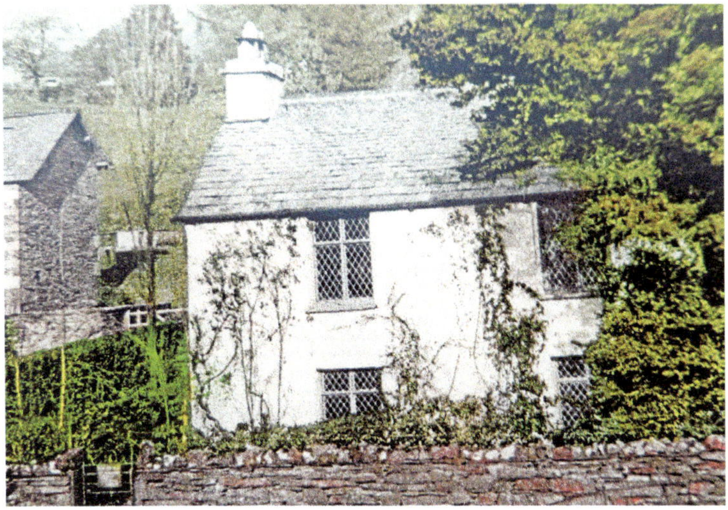

Dove Cottage

Wordsworth lived here with his sister Dorothy from 1799 until 1808. In 1802 he married Mary Hutchinson and she and her sister moved into the cottage too. Wordsworth wrote many of his famous poems whilst living here and his three children, John, Dora and Thomas, were born here. Naturally, the Wordsworth family outgrew the cottage and in 1808 they moved to larger premises. Thomas de Quincy took up residence there following their departure. A succession of tenants followed him from 1835 and eventually the Wordsworth Trust bought the cottage in 1890 for £650. The cottage was opened to the public in 1891 and has enjoyed great popularity ever since. The interior is faithful to the time when Wordsworth lived there, and the furnishings and household goods remain unchanged. The garden was returned to its wild appearance by the Trust, to reflect the preference of Wordsworth who liked a natural look. Dove Cottage has over 70,000 visitors a year and the Wordsworth Museum is adjacent to the cottage in a converted coach house. This houses documents and artefacts pertaining to Wordsworth and the Romantics and is run by the Trust as well.

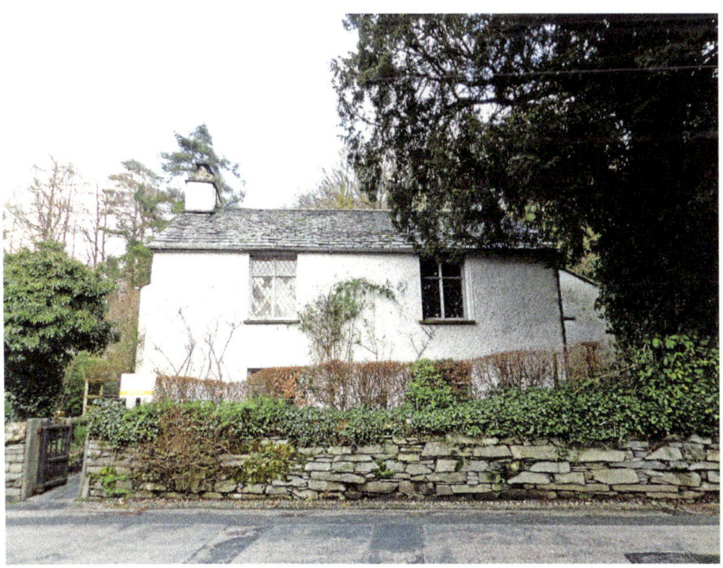

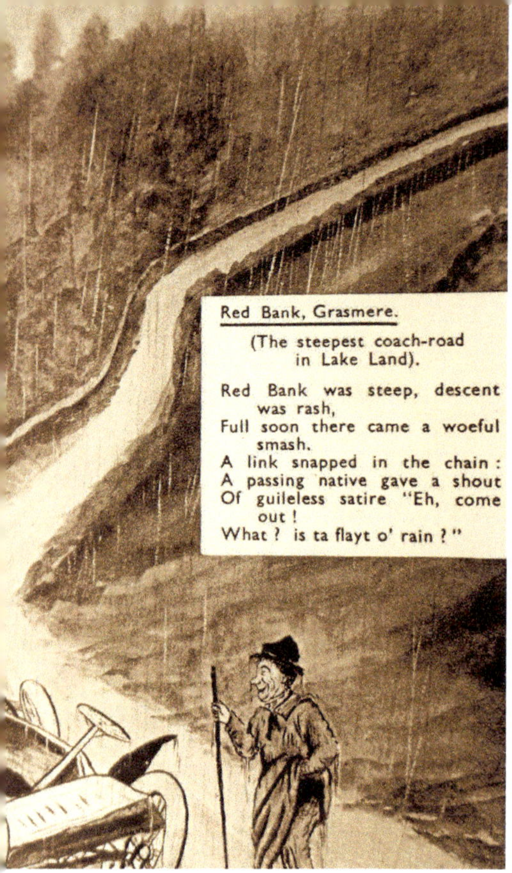

Red Bank, Grasmere

The arduous road is the subject of a humorous postcard which shows the dangers of such a steep incline while showing the local attitude to those who can't handle it. Looking over the walls and down the hillside the back of Grasmere lake is visible. It gives a good perspective of how high you are at this point and you realise it is almost 1,000 feet. There are numerous pathways that can be taken to reach the lake beach and then on to White Moss Common. It is truly beautiful in spring when the floor of the woods is carpeted in bluebells. The abundance of wildlife is amazing and if one looks carefully you might catch sight of a red squirrel or a badger.

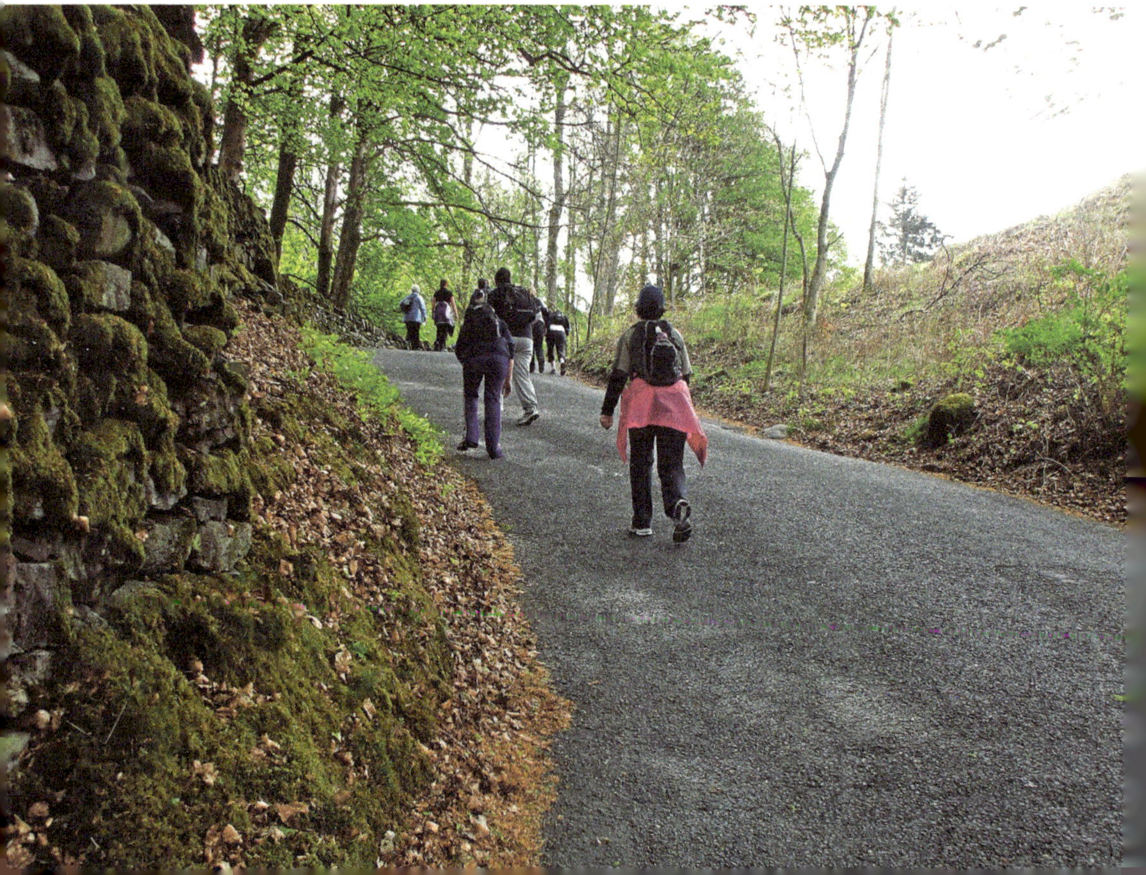

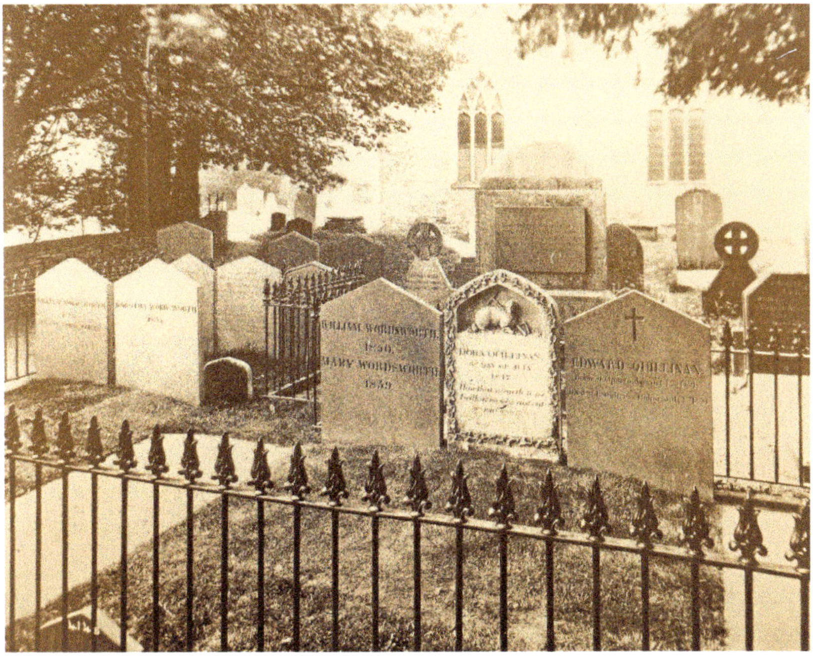

Wordsworth's Grave

This is a much-visited spot in Grasmere and the graves are unchanged, apart from age. Wordsworth died at the age of eighty – a good age for his generation – allegedly after catching a cold on one his famous walks. It seems appropriate that as one of our national poets, he died on St George's day – 23 April 1850. His wife died nine years later and is buried with him in the churchyard; in fact his whole family is buried close by, his children, sister-in-law and sister as close to him in death as they were in life. The graves are part of the Grasmere heritage trail and attract many visitors every year.

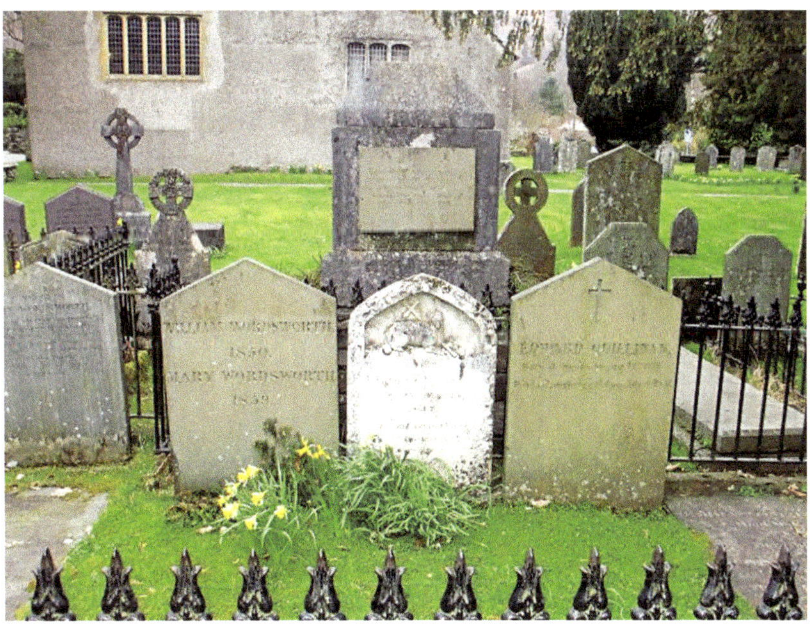

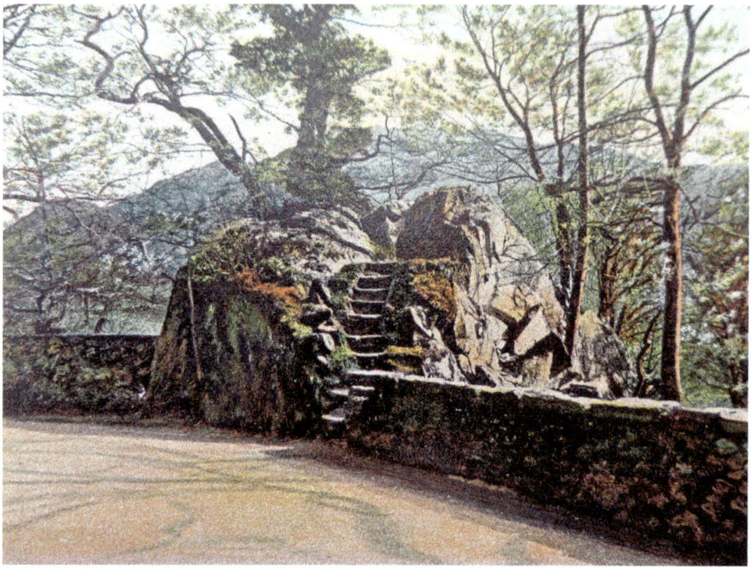

Poet's Seat, Grasmere

This romantic-sounding place is obviously closely linked to William Wordsworth. It was apparently the vantage point for his preferred view over Grasmere. It is a natural outcrop of rock, elevated above the lake and beside the road, with steps hewn into it. The photographs are far more romantic than the reality, mainly due to its position alongside the very busy road. It is hard to spot when driving past and even harder to reach unless on foot. Even then, one must be careful to find the pavement beside the wood rather than risk certain death crossing the road. The steps appear to have been reduced in number and the platform at the top has gone, leaving a rough rocky ridge. The low dry-stone wall has been removed in front and the trees have grown. The view is beautiful and on quieter moments it is easy to imagine Wordsworth taking in the view and ruminating on his next poem. I am not sure he would be quite as enamoured by it now.

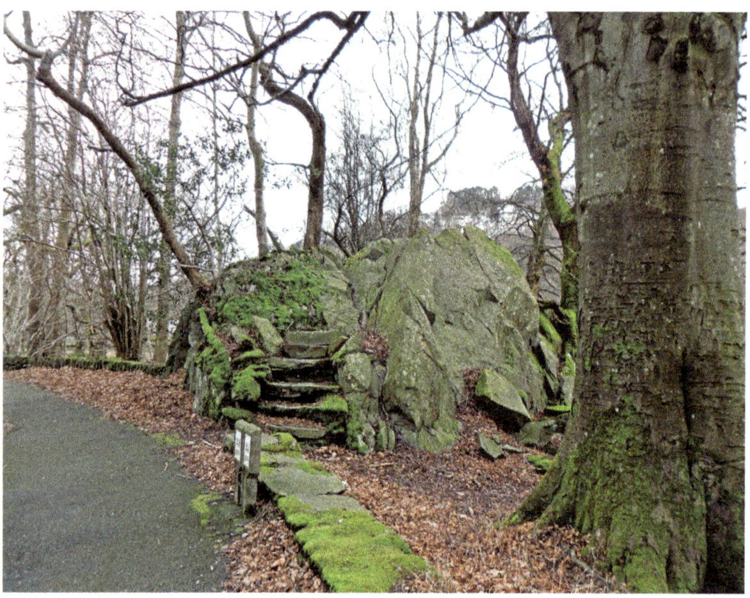

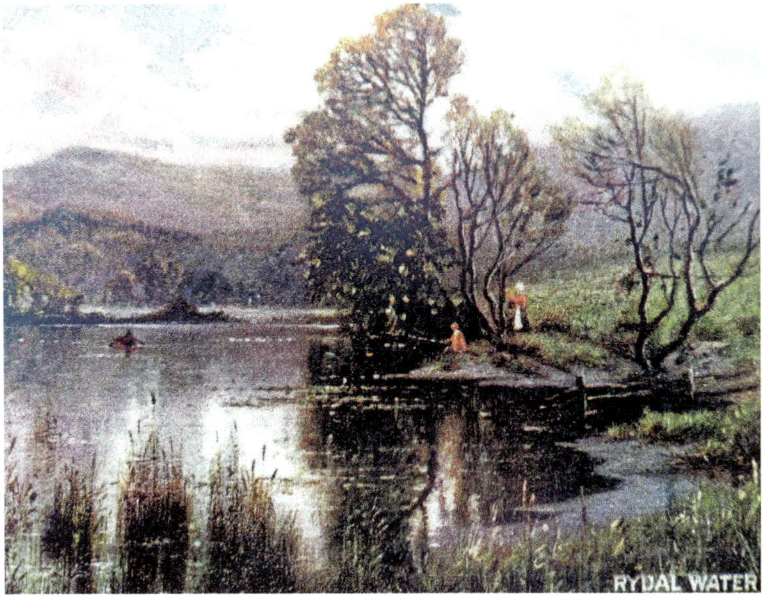

Rydal Water

The rural scene looks idyllic and peaceful, and probably was. Rydal is fed by the Rothay flowing from Grasmere and the two lakes are separated by White Moss, a wooded area popular with visitors. The fells surround the lake and the lower banks and reeds are a haven for wildlife. Rydal is one of Wordsworth's favoured spots and he frequently walked down to its banks to sit and contemplate when he lived at Rydal Mount as an old man. One can walk around the lake and the Rydal cave can be found – the remains of previous quarrying. Lowther Estates lease the southern part of Rydal to the National Trust, while the northern half is in the domain of Rydal Hall. It would be unlikely that the rowing boat would be permitted today or the children fishing. Sadly, such things are only permitted for residents of Rydal Hall nowadays.

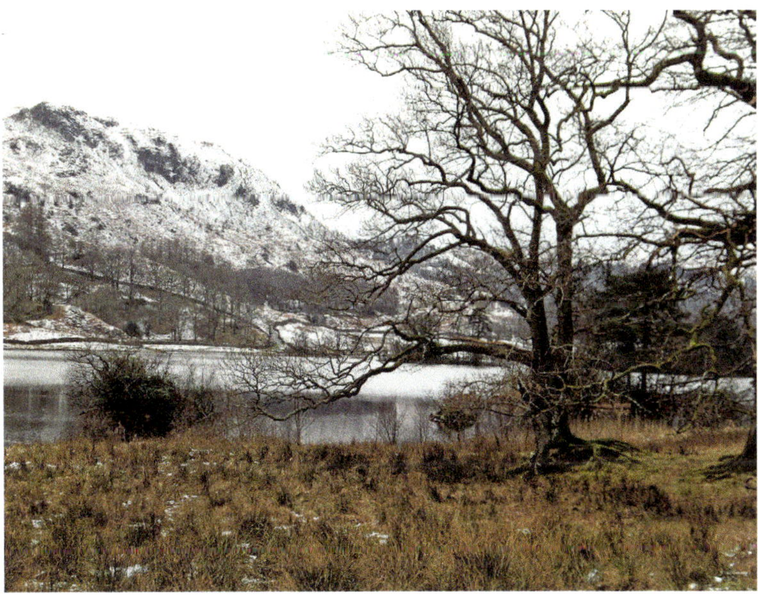

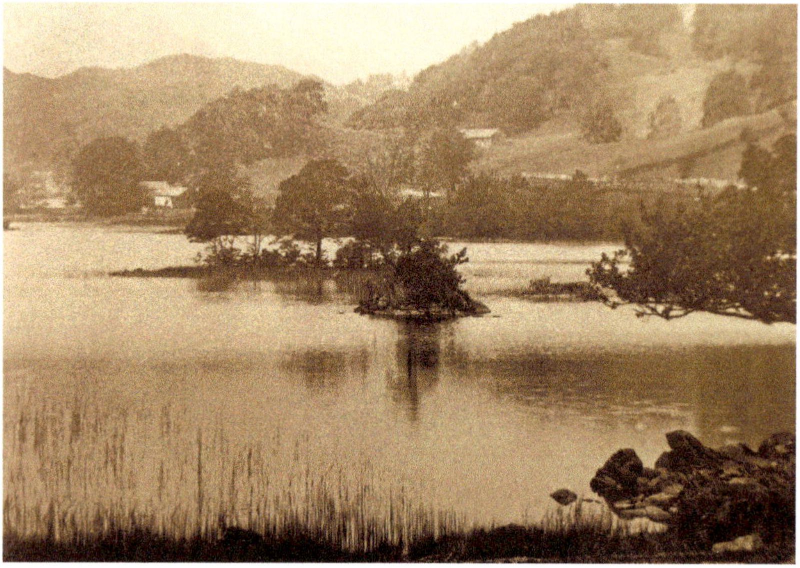

Rydal Water, Nab Cottage

The small lake was favoured by the Romantics and painters alike and many spent time here in the nineteenth century. Nab Cottage is famous as the home, for a time, of Thomas de Quincy, Wordsworth's friend, and later Hartley Coleridge, the son of Samuel Taylor Coleridge. The area in Wordsworth's time had been principally agricultural, but ironically, although he railed against change and the development of the Lake District, he was one of the main progenitors, as it was his poems that attracted them. Rydal has a small hamlet at its head and there are a variety of hotels and inns, but it has not yet been exploited completely for the tourist trade. One wonders how long this will be so, considering some of the suggested plans for White Moss Common, between Rydal and Grasmere, such as the 'visitor hub' which Lowther Estates favoured. Luckily, this unsullied woodland walk was saved by the local planning department denying permission for this to be built.

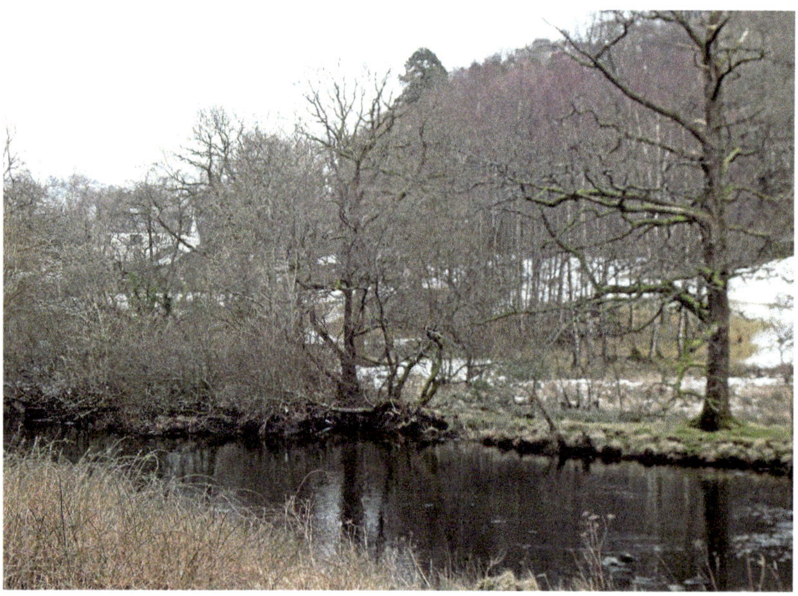

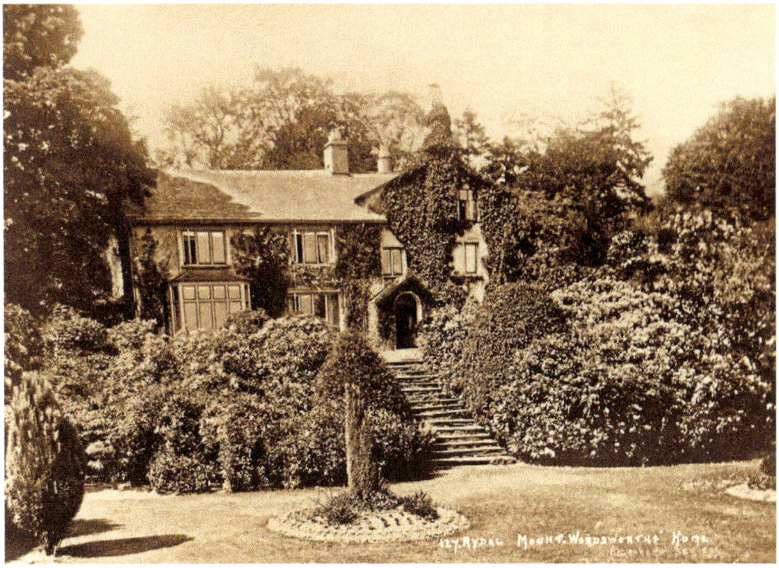

Rydal Mount

Wordsworth's final home is surrounded by landscaped gardens overlooking the lake and the fells. He lived there from 1813 until 1850 and he took immense pride in the grounds. Naturally, daffodils feature in the area. On his daughter's death in 1847 Wordsworth planted hundreds of bulbs to commemorate her. This is now called Dora's field and is held by the National Trust. Although Wordsworth had a large study, he spent his time in the grounds and he built a writing hut in which he spent a lot of his time. He had regular visitors including Samuel Taylor Coleridge. He edited and wrote parts of his autobiographical *Prelude* and some of his most famous poems. The house was rented from Lady Le Fleming of Rydal Hall by the Wordsworth family until after his death until 1859. Later his great-great-granddaughter Mary Henderson acquired the property in 1969 and it remains in the Wordsworth family.

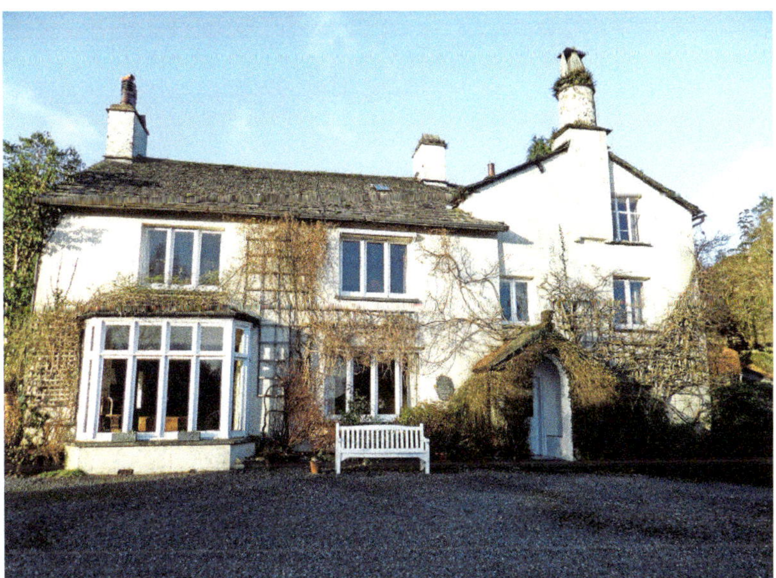

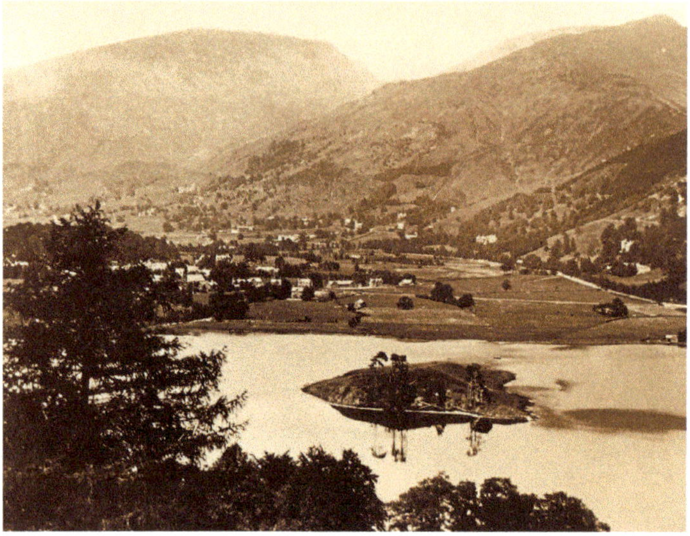

Grasmere and Village

The village of Grasmere is one of the prettiest, seated as it is at the head of the lake. The dramatic hills surrounding it are evocatively named. Helm Crag is known locally as the 'lion and the lamb' looking north, or the 'old lady playing a piano' looking south, which can be clearly seen in the modern photograph. High Raise, Blea Rigg, Silver How and the Fairfield Horseshoe are the other fells well known to walkers and ramblers. The village is bisected by the River Rothay and is nestled within a triangle of roads. This place, above all, has retained its original look to some extent, albeit targeting the tourist audience. The buildings are typically Lakeland and some of the shops and hotels reflect the rural nature of the area. Naturally, the Wordsworth effect is strongest here, Wordsworth having lived in Grasmere for fourteen years. The church is a place of pilgrimage for the Wordsworth enthusiast, his family grave located in the churchyard. There is much to see and discover here and the views from any place are spectacular. The view on the two photographs are at contrasting times of the year, but the contrast shows the beauty remains all year round. As Wordsworth said himself it is 'the loveliest spot that man hath ever found'.

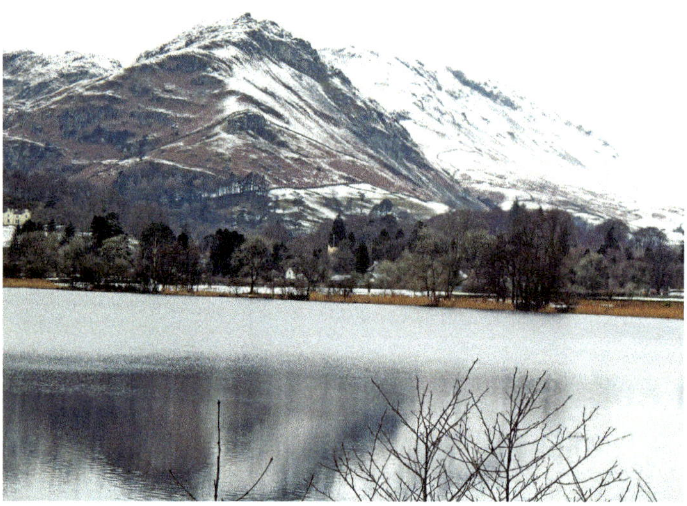

Grasmere Church

The church has become a place of pilgrimage for visitors because of the Wordsworth family graves. The Wordsworth legacy continues around St Oswald's Church through a Daffodil Walk, sponsored by and designed for the Friends of Wordsworth. The path is built on church land and the sponsored commemorative paving slabs helped to fund the upkeep of the church. The scheme continues, and a wild daffodil can be planted in memory of a loved one as a tangible marker of their presence on earth. At the same time there is the satisfaction of knowing you are helping to support the upkeep of the church. The slate path is in keeping with the surroundings and this leads to a tranquil area where one can sit and contemplate in the shadow of the great man's resting place.

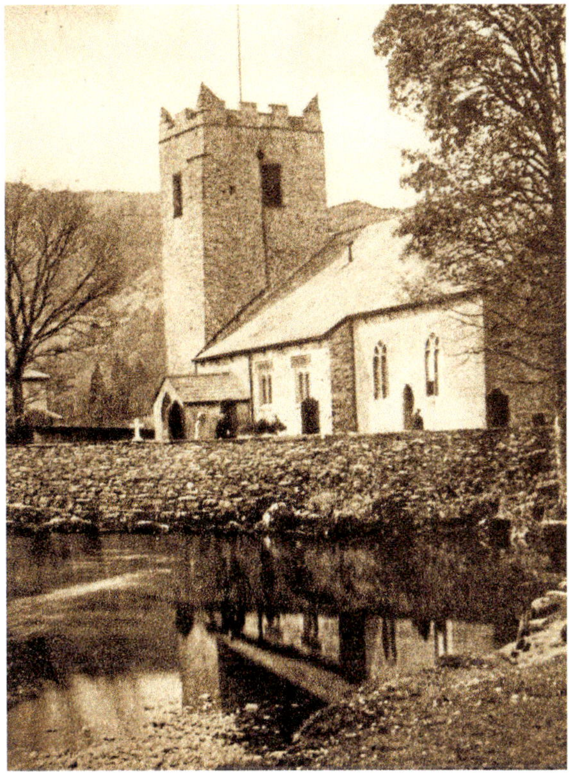

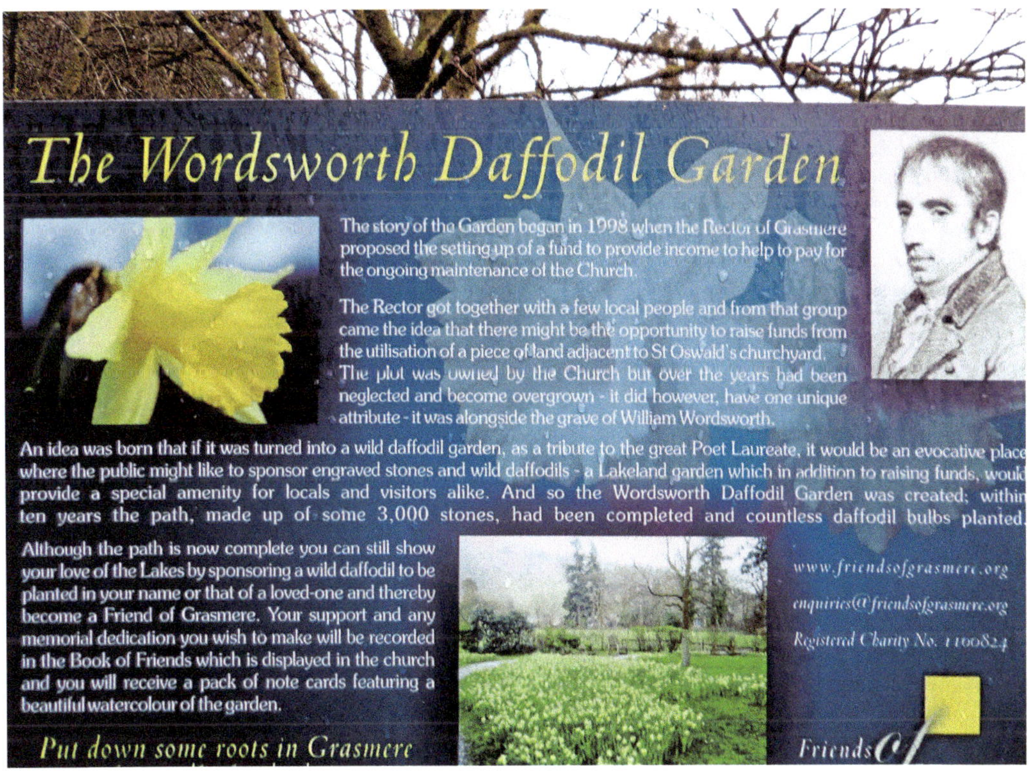

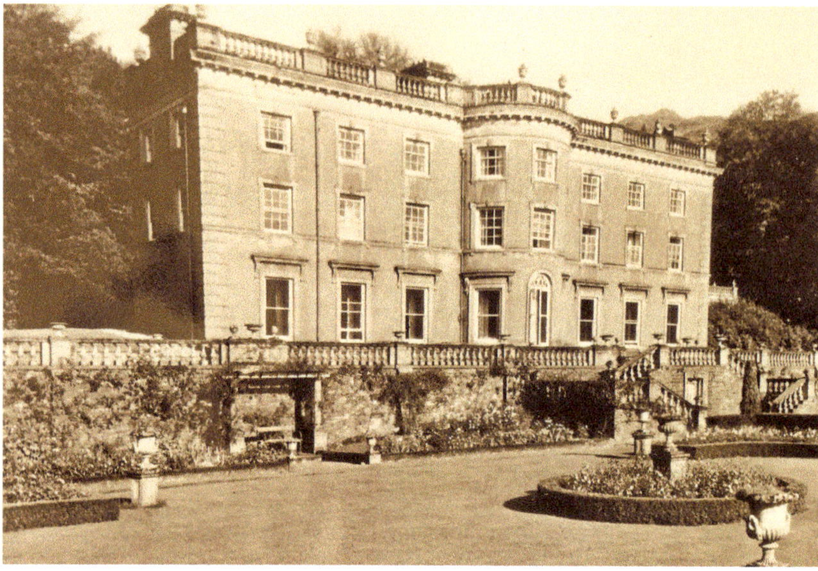

Rydal Hall

This beautiful country house was the seat of the Le Fleming family until 1970, when the house and gardens were sold to the Diocese of Carlisle. The rest of the estate remained in Le Fleming hands until 1998. The earliest house was built in the sixteenth century but has had many adaptations since. In the nineteenth century the façade we see today was created and it is an obvious landmark in the surrounding countryside. The gardens were designed by Sir Thomas Mawson and they hold many surprises for the visitor, such as the 'Grot', Rydal Falls, and Italianate terraces surrounded by verdant woodland. Wordsworth lived above the hall at Rydal Mount, renting it from Lady Fleming until his death and was familiar with the gardens and woods. The hall participates in 'Wordsworth's Daffodil Legacy' devised by the National Gardens Scheme, providing an open day to raise funds for charity. It is a retreat and conference centre now and has a tea room and holiday accommodation. Many artists and writers have stayed here, and it is part of the Wordsworth cultural trail.

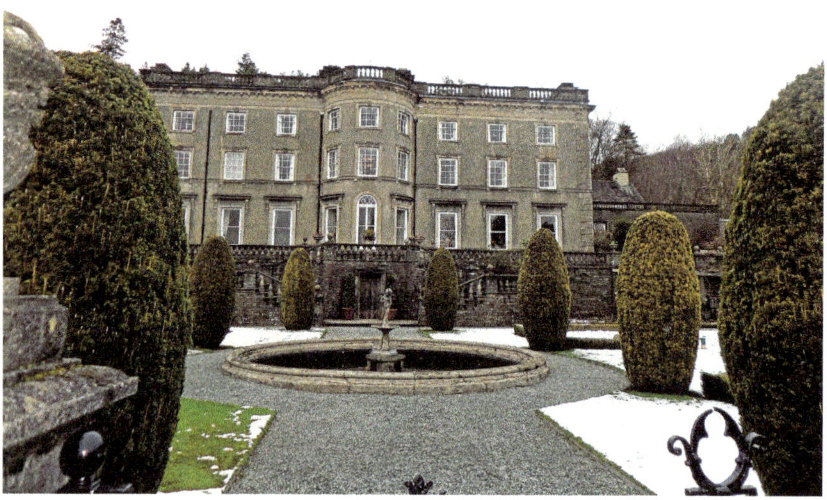

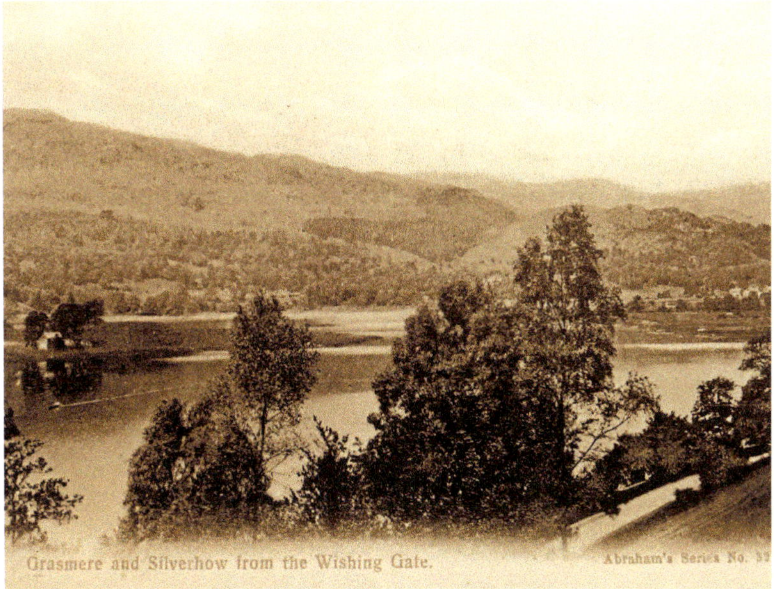

Grasmere

The depiction of Grasmere on this Abrahams series postcard is another attractive view towards the village. The Abraham brothers were enthusiastic climbers who lived in Keswick in the nineteenth and early twentieth centuries. They were pioneering rock climbers who are also remembered for their valuable photographic records of early mountaineers. They owned a photographic shop in Keswick and produced popular postcards for visitors, showing many of the iconic Lake District views we still recognise today. The quality and sharpness of the photographs is remarkable considering how primitive photographic processes were at the time. Grasmere and Rydal were just two of the lakes the Abrahams photographed, and we are in their debt for recording the Lakes in its unspoilt state.

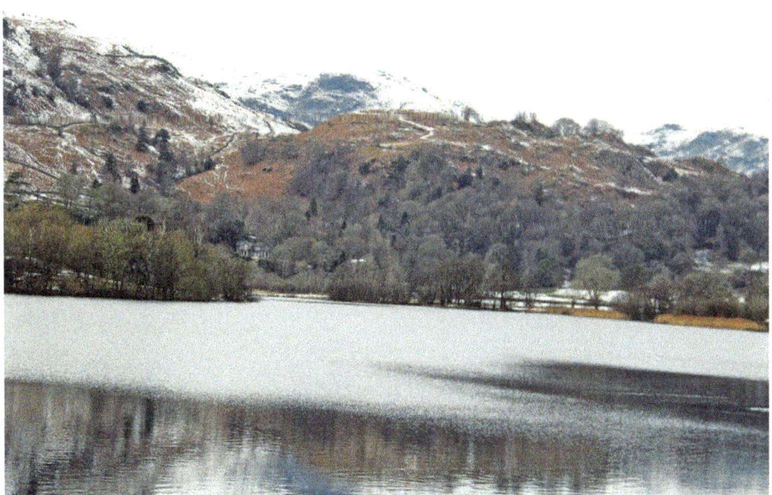

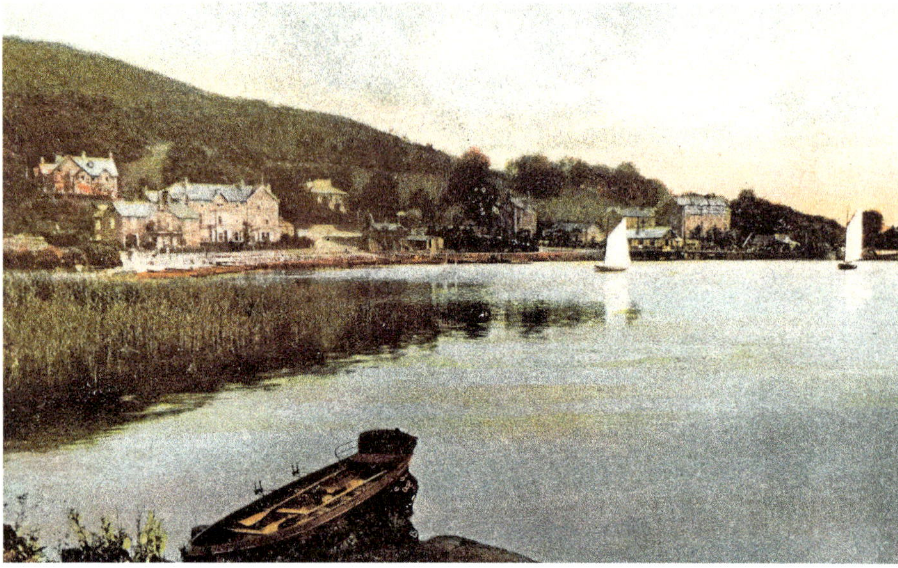

Waterhead, Ambleside

Looking towards Waterhead one can see some urban growth and development, but many of the buildings in the postcard are still present. Waterhead is the destination for the pleasure steamers and the pier is much the same. The lake ends here and is around a mile from the village itself. It is a strategic point and one can understand why the Roman fort was built here, for easy access to the lake and as a staging post to the north. The Waterhead Hotel has grown and therefore so has its visual impact, presenting a very prominent image along the lakeside. Once again it has been modernised; some original features remain but it is now termed a 'boutique hotel'. Outside there is a plethora of signage advertising the facilities, often unnecessarily. I am unsure that the commendation from the *Telegraph,* 'a slick bolthole with the prettiest views', would fulfil my idea of the archetypal Lakes hotel, but to many it must, as this is a very popular and attractive hotel.

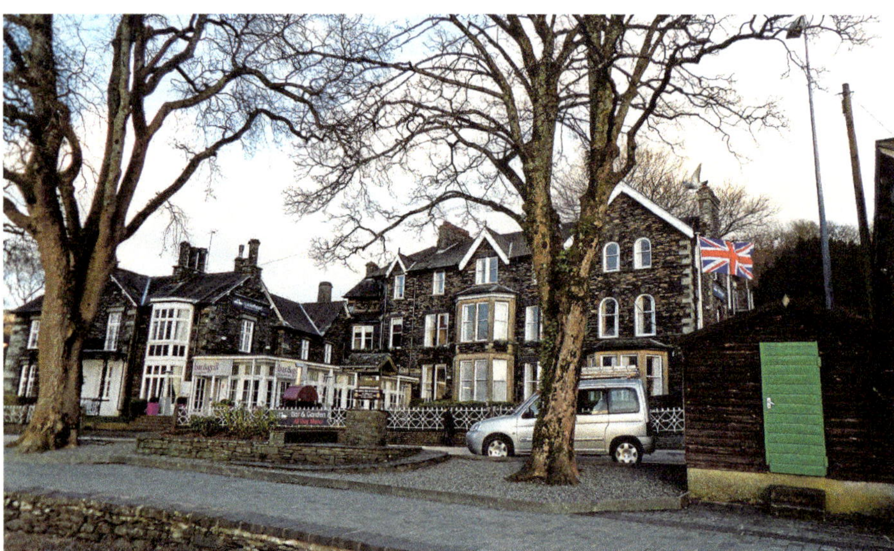

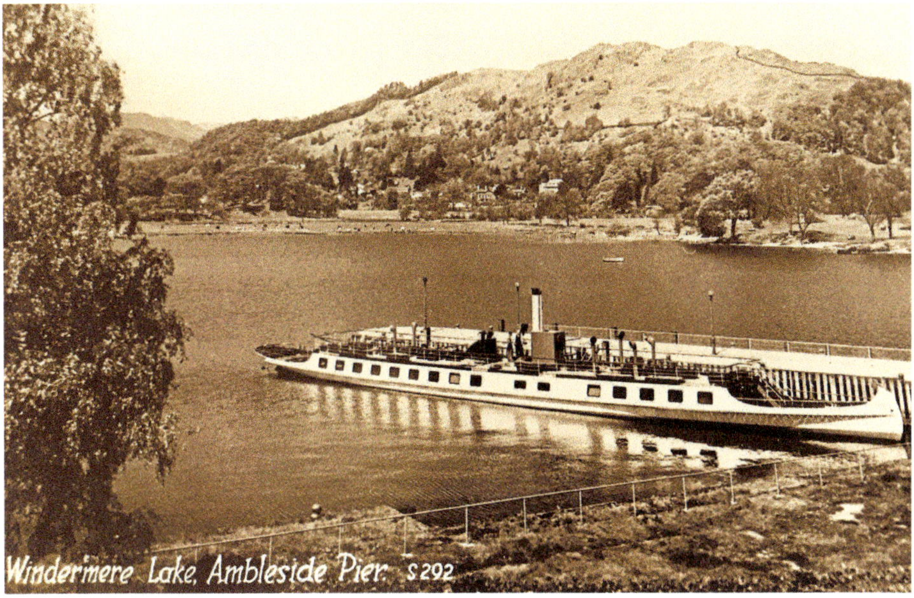

Ambleside Pier

Transport in the Lake District has always included services along the lake. Waterhead has several piers, some which are now privately owned. The steamer service has terminated here for many years and the pier is an attractive Gothic building that is still intact. The ticket office is in the same style as its counterparts at Bowness. The boat pictured is SY *Tern*, one of the steamboats that traversed the length of Lake Windermere from the 1890s onwards. The area around the pier was sparsely populated and only the Toll House, the Grange, Waterhead and Wateredge Hotels were much smaller and were originally a farm. The waterfront is still pleasant with amazing views across the lake. Borrans Road runs beside it and the area behind the Waterhead has been extensively developed with hotels and houses, and the road runs into the village from here.

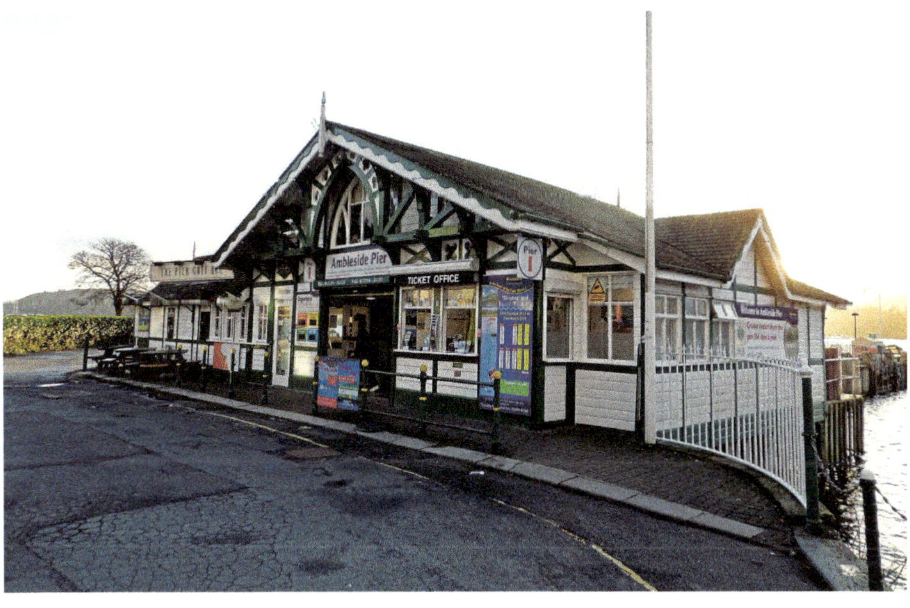

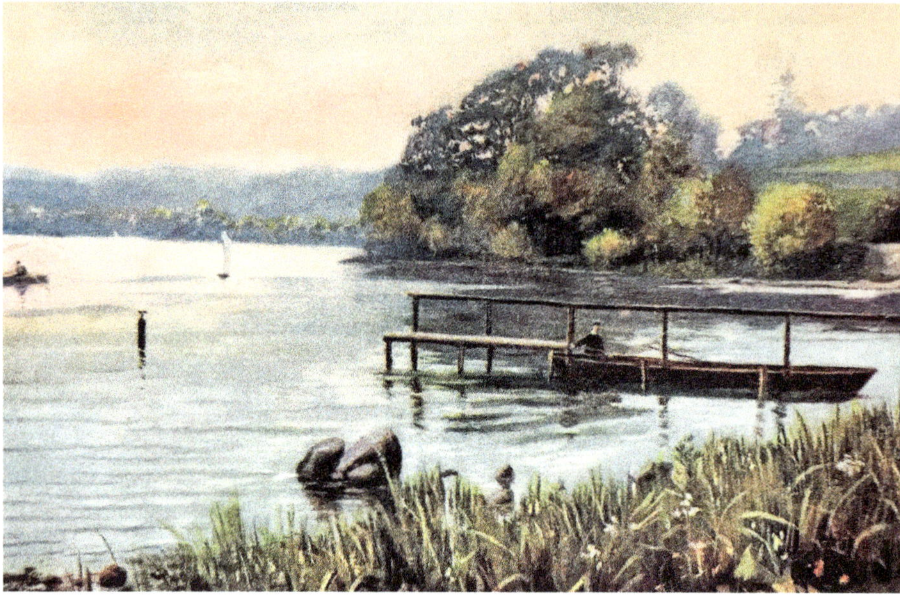

Waterhead, Ambleside

The two photographs here are very similar on first appraisal but when one takes a closer look there are some significant changes. The scenes are looking over the lake towards Borrans Park where the Roman fort is situated. The piers and banks in the old photograph are of a rural nature and appear quite natural. In the second one we can see that the aspect is much more ordered and sophisticated. The beach is bounded by slate-edged pathways and neat gated piers for private use. The yachts are moored close by and are privately owned. The buildings have increased down the length of the road and it has become semi-residential or given over to holidaymakers. Borrans Road is a busy one and adjoins the Lake Road at the traffic lights. This becomes very congested in the peak season, and tranquillity then is more difficult to find.

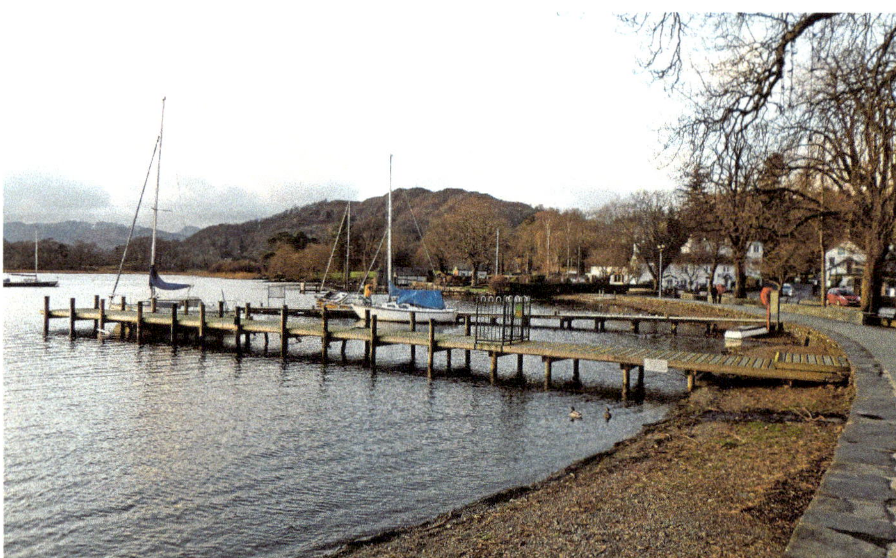

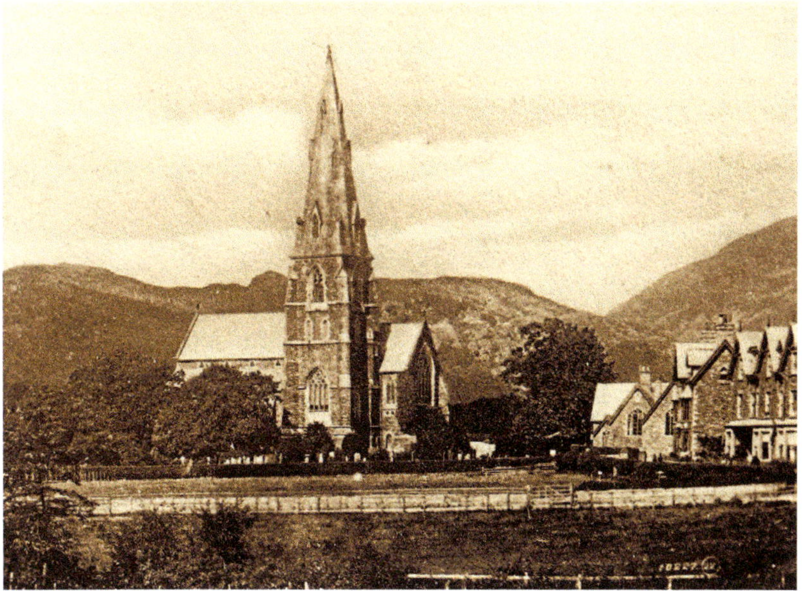

Ambleside Church

St Mary's Church was designed and built by Sir George Gilbert Scott in 1854. This was to increase accommodation for the growth of the congregation at the old church. Windows are dedicated to the Wordsworth family and a chapel was established in 1952 dedicated to them. The church took four years to complete, the spire rising to 180 feet. There is a wall painting of the famous Rush Bearing ceremony by George Ransom inside created in 1944. The mural was given as a thank you from the Royal Academy of Art for the time they spent in Ambleside as evacuees during the Second World War. The church is well kept, and the graveyard holds the remains of the famous educationalist Charlotte Mason who established a training college of the same name in the village. It is still an active part of the community and is well placed in the middle of the village.

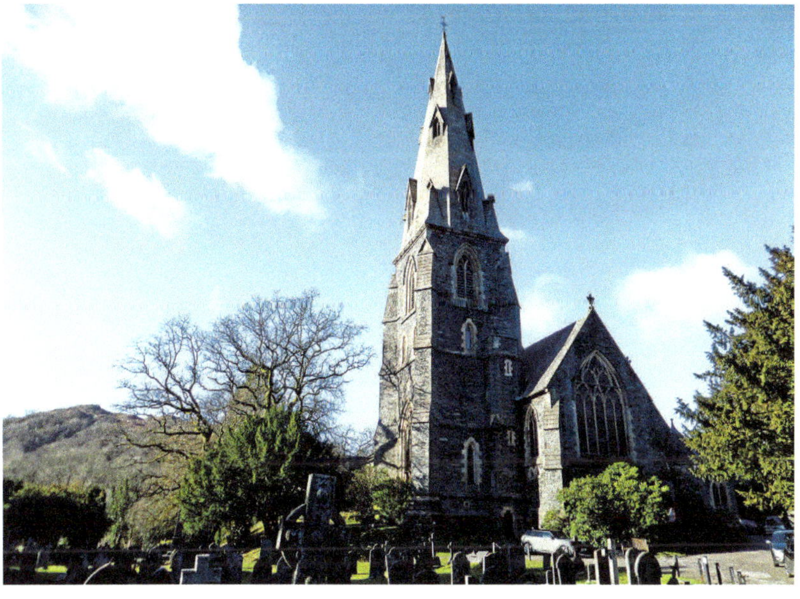

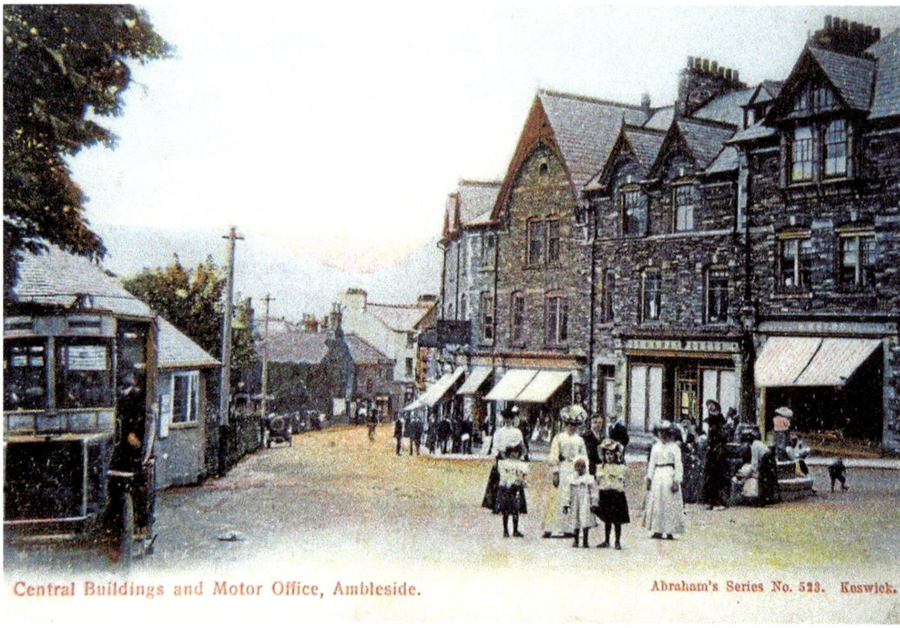

Ambleside Main Street

This charming Edwardian view of the main street and Central Buildings in Ambleside was captured in the Abrahams series of postcards. Motor traffic is sparse, though we can see a bus outside the new bus station and a car parked in the street lower down. Pedestrians stand unperturbed in the road and congregate in front of the shops. The market cross is visible in both pictures and there are shoppers on the pavements. The shops no longer sport their awnings in the modern version and cars are more numerous, as is the extent and variety of street signage, road markings and street furniture. The buildings still house small businesses, most of them targeting visitors rather than the local shoppers.

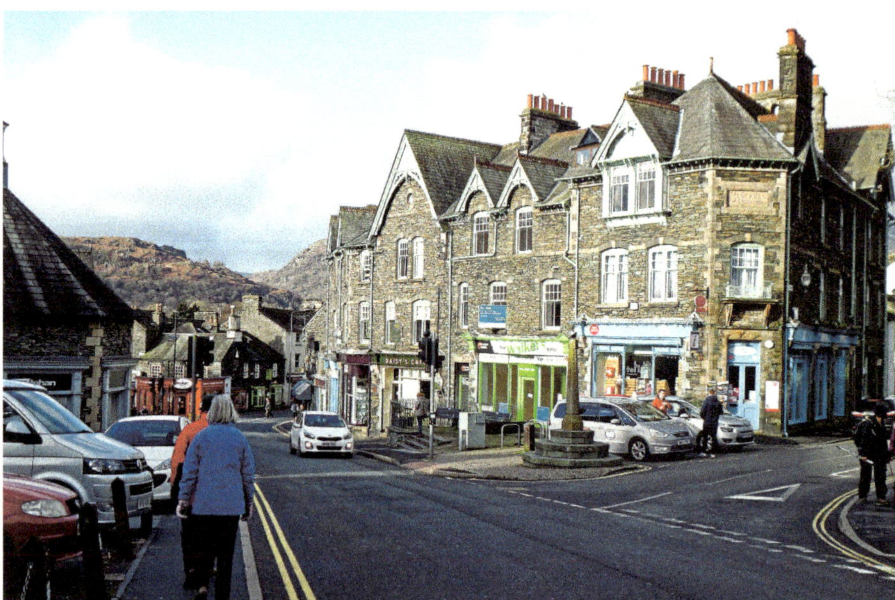

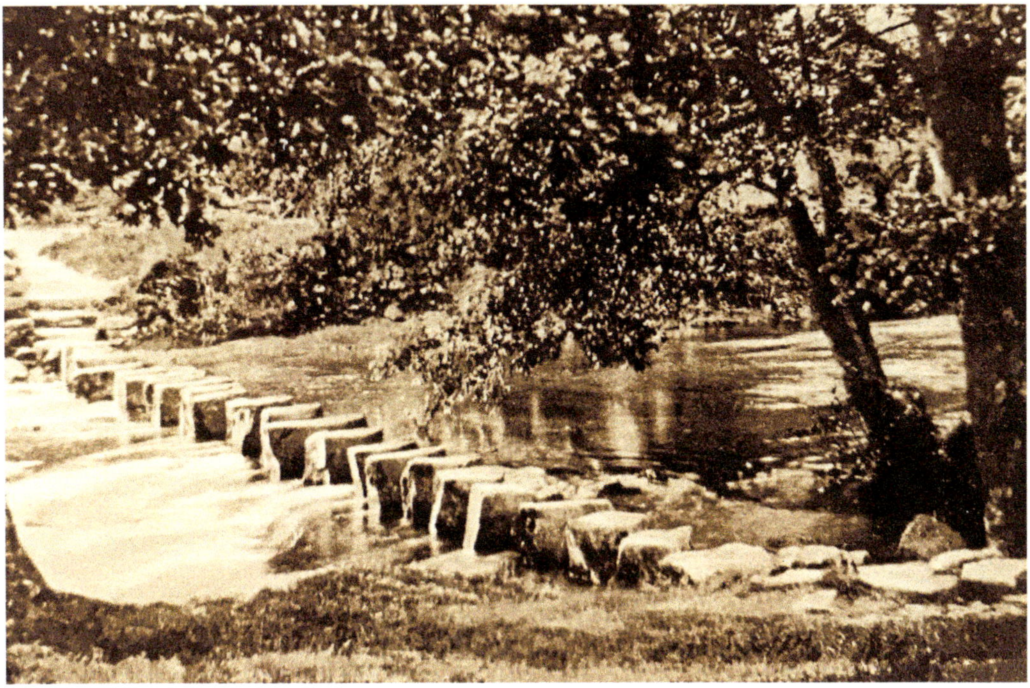

Stepping Stones, Ambleside

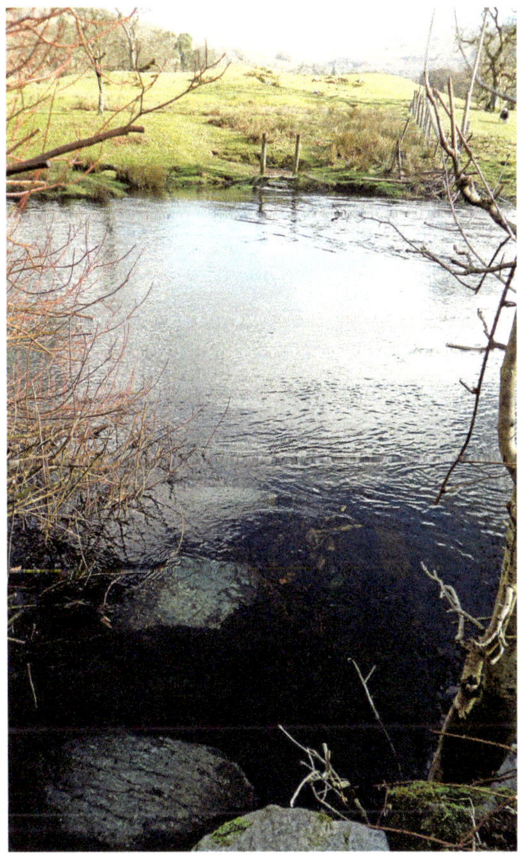

Another prominent location on the Wordsworth trail, the Stepping Stones across the Rothay was somewhere I was looking forward to visiting. The stones, long established as a preferred route from Ambleside to Grasmere by Dorothy Wordsworth, cross the river at Pelter Bridge. The card is an evocative one, producing a rural and picturesque view of these ancient stones and the location is easily found. However, on arrival, the guest house of the same name was obvious, but the Stepping Stones were not. It took a few moments to realise what had happened. The stones were entirely covered by the river, presumably due to the extra water from the melting snow in the hills, but although those at the bank were visible, there were very few in the middle of the river. Sadly, due to severe storms and floods in the autumn, the central stones were washed away and all that is left are a few on either side and the posts marking where they start. The surrounding countryside and the views are still beautiful, but the stones have disappeared, possibly forever.

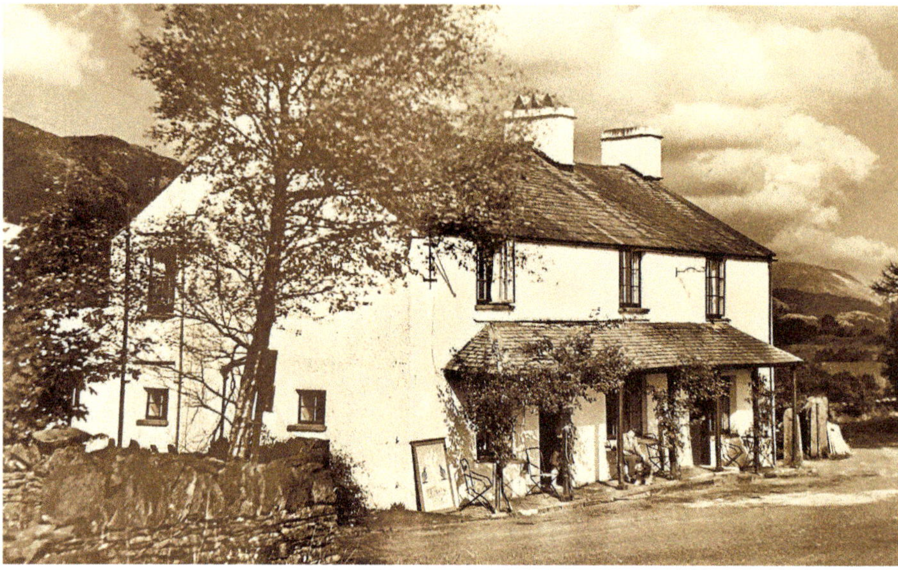

Drunken Duck, Ambleside

A novel name with a novel tale; the veracity of the tale is up to the reader to decide. Apparently, a previous landlady of the pub in the nineteenth century discovered her flock of ducks had drunk water contaminated with ale which had leaked into the supply. They were all unconscious and she thought they had died. Rather than waste the ducks she began to pluck them ready for the table. However, they were not dead, just intoxicated and slowly they awoke. The story becomes even more interesting because the landlady, feeling very upset and guilty, knitted them all waistcoats to cover their featherless bodies made from Hawkshead yarn. Sadly, there is no photographic evidence of this, so it must be left to the imagination to conjure up an image. The pub is typical of those in Lakeland and sits at a crossroads. Although modernised to be acceptable for the contemporary visitor, it retains its rustic character and is filled with prints and artefacts echoing its past. Its oak floors, wooden settles and Herdwick wool coverings all create an authentic atmosphere and appearance.

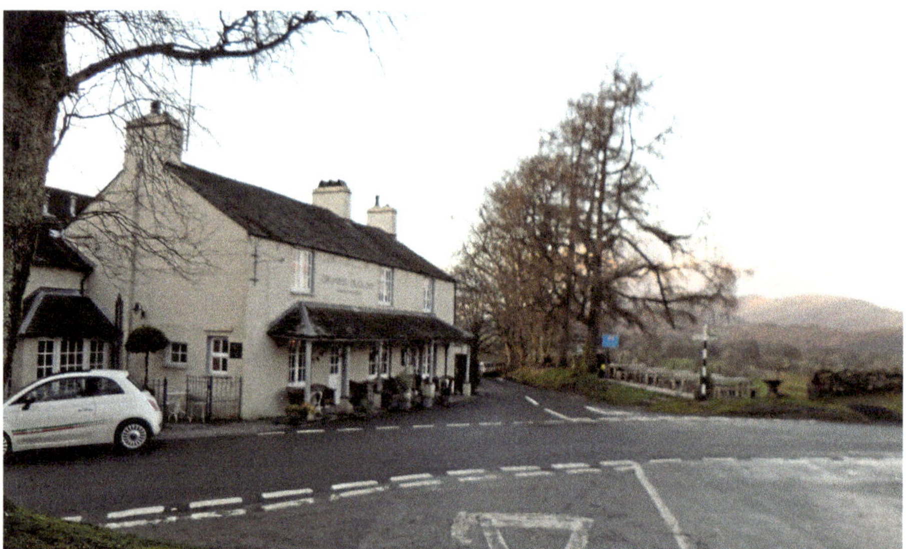

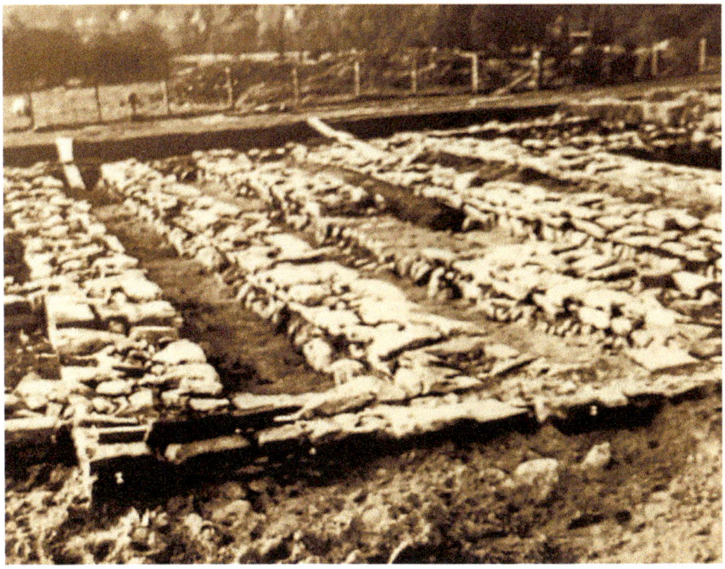

Ambleside Roman Fort

The Romans built a timber garrison at Ambleside at the end of the first century AD, which housed 200 men. Although it was abandoned it was later reoccupied, this time being built in stone on a raised platform. One speculates this might have been because of flooding as the field in which it sits is very boggy even today. Galava was one of several staging forts in the Lake District and there were 500 infantrymen based here; there was a grain store and it would have been on the supply route north, being well placed on the edge of the lake. The fort remained in use till the fourth century AD and a settlement grew around it. The fort is partially exposed, and there are information boards and viewing platforms around the site; however, it is often overlooked, and many people are surprised to discover its existence. Today certain features can be seen, such as the *Principia* or headquarters, the *Horrea* or granaries, and the *Praetorium* where the commanding officer lived. Other evidence such as the gateways and towers can also be found. The fort is nestled in Gorran's Field near the park and often has livestock wandering across it. It is administered jointly by English Heritage and the National Trust.

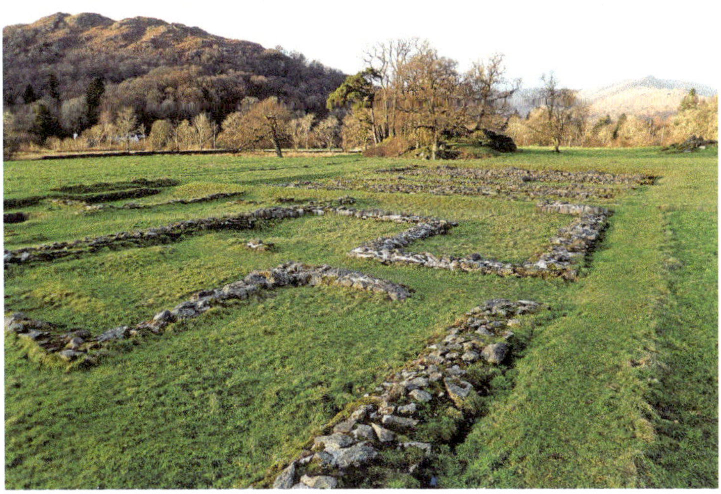

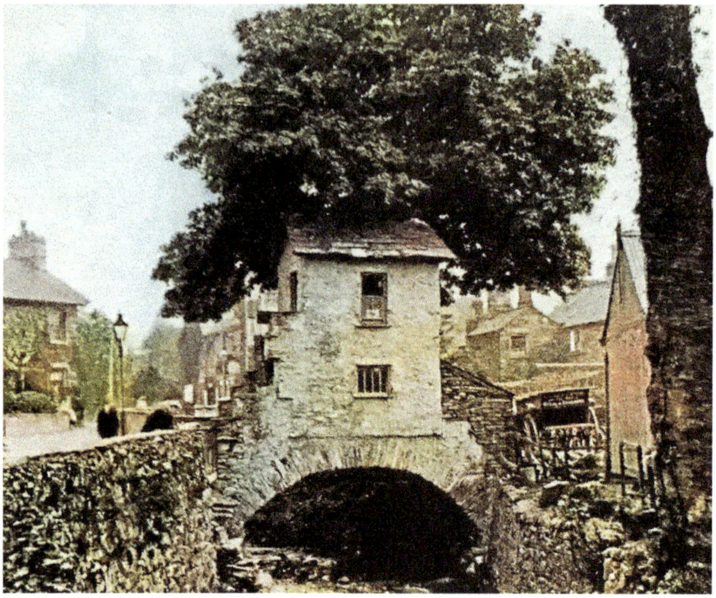

Ambleside Bridge House

Probably one of the most iconic views in the Lakes, the Bridge House is admired by all who see it. The National Trust look after it and it sits over Stock Gill Beck as it always has done. It's a tiny house made from slate in the traditional way and was apparently built as a garden house for Ambleside Hall. The house was occupied in the 1850s by Chairy Rigg, a basket-maker who managed to rear a family of six in this diminutive building. None of the modern facilities were available, such as running water and sanitation, but this didn't appear to affect the family. It has been painted and drawn by many artists including Turner and is a definitive landmark in Ambleside. The house was donated to the National Trust in 1926 and was one of their earliest recruiting centres. It is very close to the main road and at high season is crowded with visitors and people taking photographs of it. A replica can be seen at Hayes Garden Centre, at the other end of Ambleside.

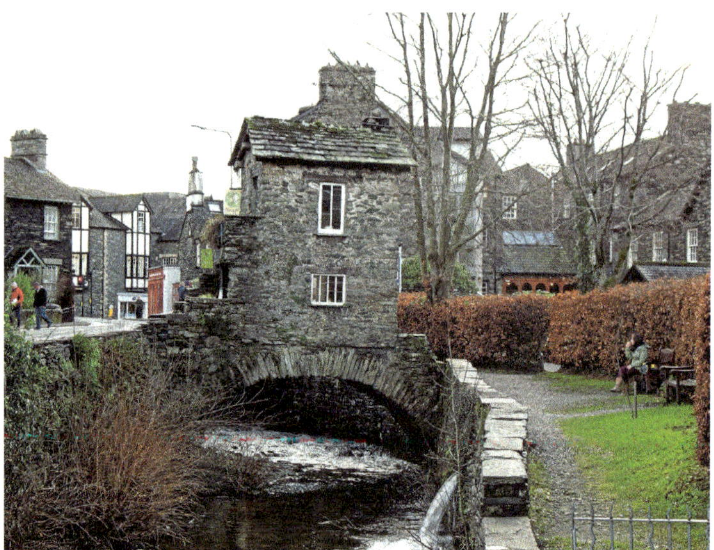

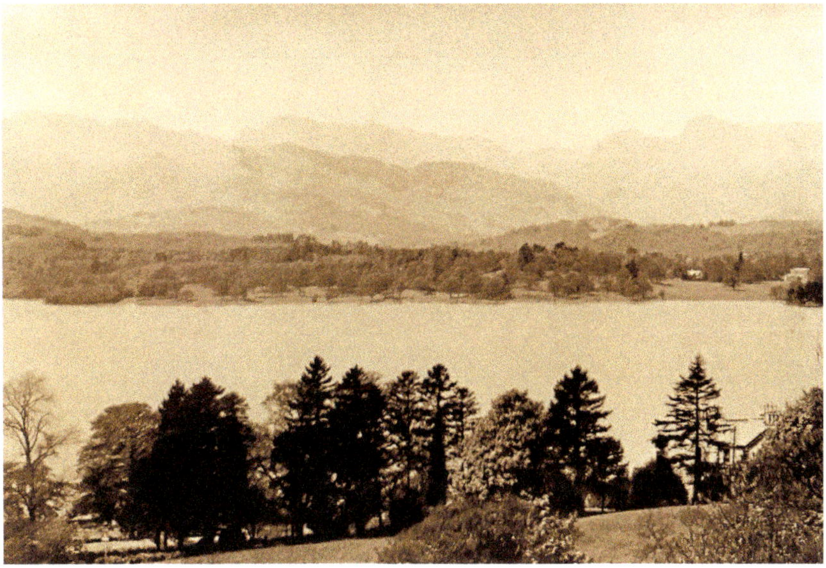

View towards Langdale

The two views of Windermere that reveal the dramatic backdrop of the Langdales. The views are very similar and show a typical lake aspect, with conifers and the fells rising above. The earlier picture does not indicate where it was taken, but the modern one is from Brockhole looking north-west. The Langdale Pikes are easily identified and are popular climbing destinations. On the Langdale screes there are the remains of a Neolithic axe factory. The axes are distinctive, made from greenstone volcanic tuff, the finished articles highly polished over many hours. These are found all over Europe and were traded, possibly as ritual or status symbols. The hillside is littered with fragments, chippings and unfinished or imperfect axes which have been quarried from remote and inhospitable areas such as the Pike o' Stickle and Harrison Stickle, some above 2,000 to 3,000 feet up. Some efforts have been made to conserve the sites by the National Trust, and English Heritage have discussed practical options for safe management of these important locations.

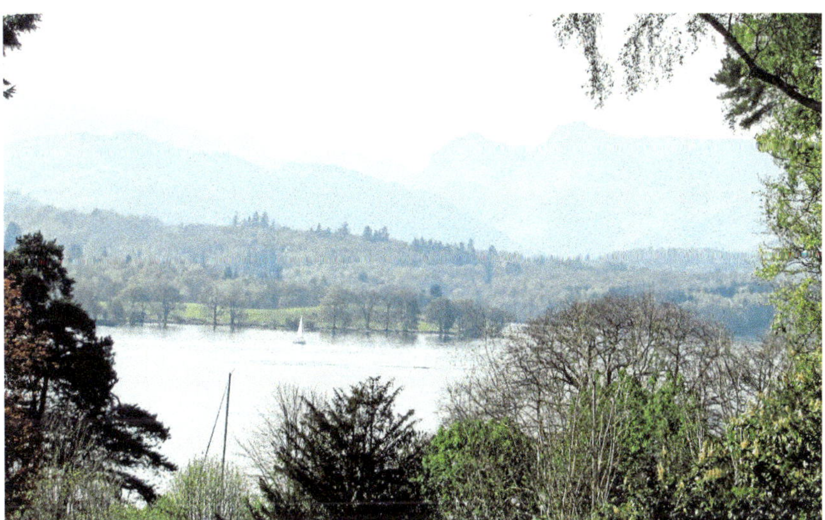

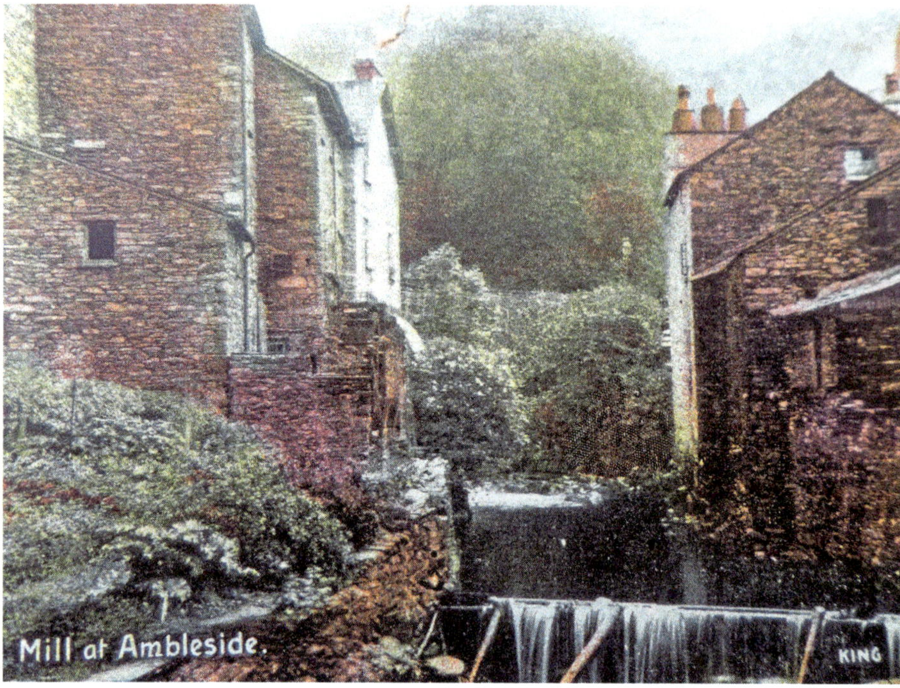

Mill at Ambleside

Stock Gill was always important in the industrial activity of Ambleside, the force of the water providing power and energy. The original lakeside settlement of the Romans was moved inland by the time of the Norse settlers. It was a farming community and the power of the beck was soon harnessed. A mill was established in 1335 and subsequent mills followed, grinding grain principally and later used for the wool industry – washing, fulling and weaving. The mill continued into the eighteenth century. Later, the mills were important in other industry arising from coppicing, such as crushing bark to make tannin for the curing of skins. The mill is still evident and the area surrounding it is well conserved, giving a very clear impression of the past. New businesses have occupied the buildings and visitors can stroll through the ginnels and explore times gone by.

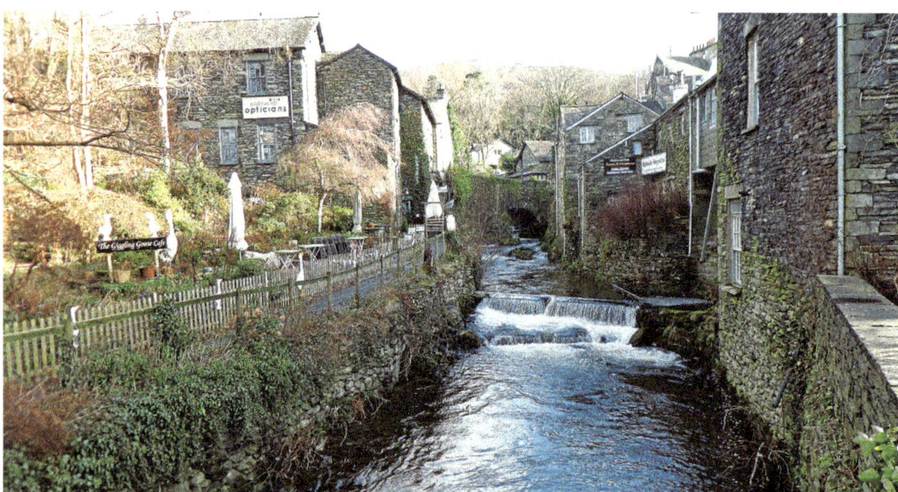

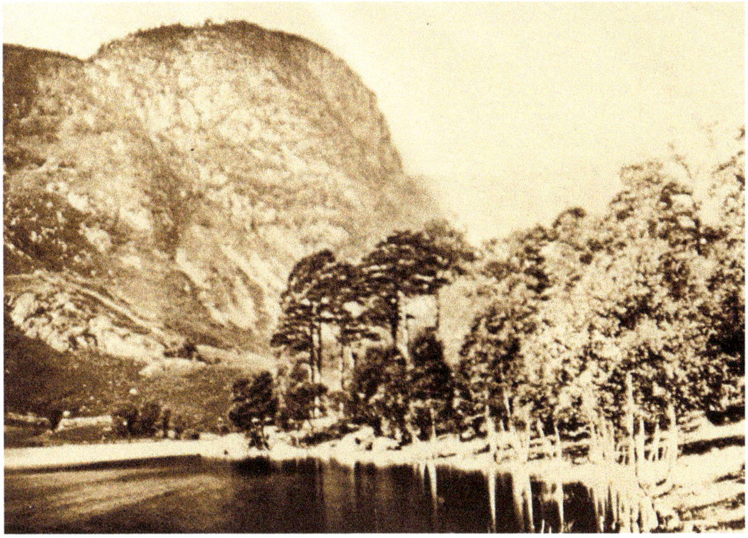

Thirlmere before the Dam

A small mention must be made of Thirlmere, which is a few miles away from Grasmere. This lake is a major reservoir that supplies Manchester with water. The lake is over 3 miles in length and over a mile wide, and its depth can reach 158 feet when full. It was originally two small lakes, and these were dammed to flood the valley and produce the body of water we see today. There was opposition to the scheme by the Manchester City Corporation Works in 1889 but the plan prevailed. Ruskin, who although in favour of social reform, was not impressed by this plan to provide Manchester with drinking water at the expense of two villages and a valley. The lake is 4 miles long and 2 miles across and to those who are unaware of its origin provides a picturesque and attractive vista. Amboth and Wythburn disappeared beneath the waters but Wythburn church and a few cottages remain at the southern end. Helvellyn can be reached from here and Wordsworth, Sir Walter Scott and Humphrey Davy made the ascent from this point. The lakeside was planted with conifers from 1908 onwards and had a rather stiff appearance initially. However, this Scandinavian appearance is slowly giving way to softer, broad-leafed species and looks more natural.

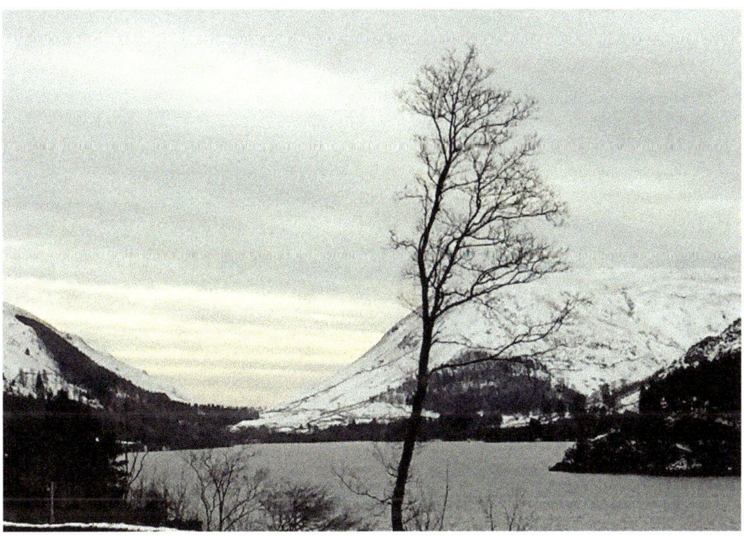

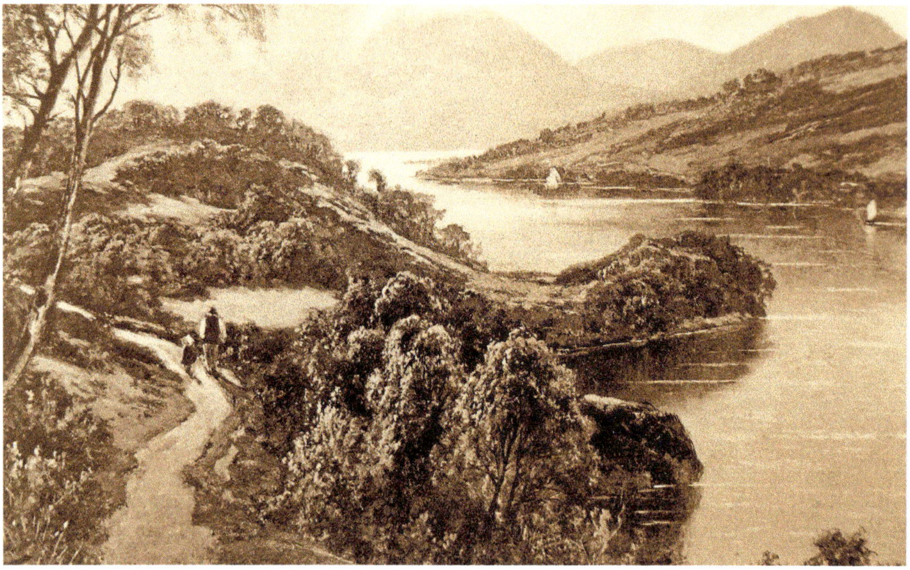

Thirlmere

The controversial dam has a commemorative stone bearing the date work was begun, 22 August 1890. Currently, the mere belongs to United Utilities and there are many lay-bys and small car parks to facilitate visitors along the western side. It is stunningly beautiful, and one can forget the man-made aspect of the place. The views are ever changing and are most spectacular in May when the woods are full of bluebells and the light plays through the green leaves and on the water. On a Saturday in May the peace of the lake is disturbed by upwards of 2,000 walkers and runners participating in the Keswick to Barrow walk of 40 miles. The beauty of the place ameliorates the necessary early 5.30 a.m. start and is a lovely way to begin the day. The lake in recent years has suffered from both drought and heavy bouts of precipitation. The steep wooded sides are full of wildlife, including the charming but endangered red squirrel. The red squirrel is now protected, and the northern lakes is one of the few places it can be found.

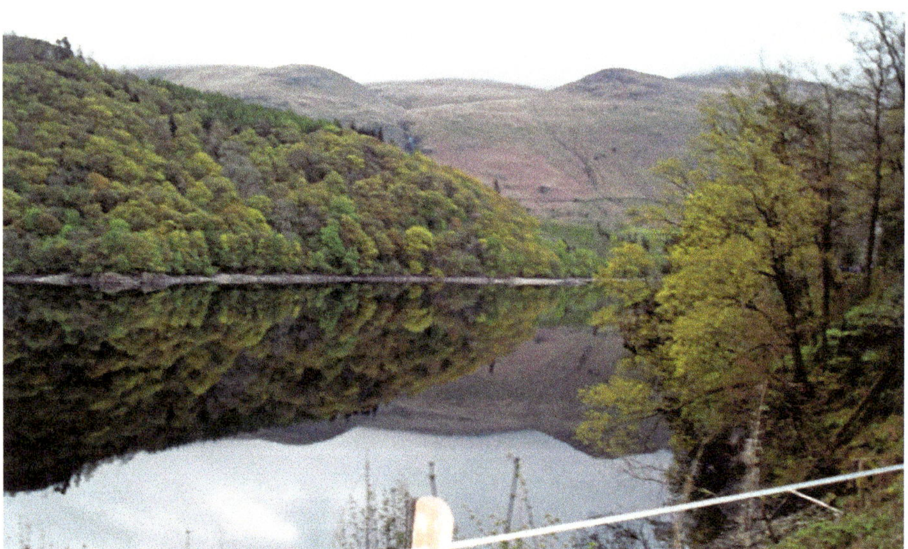

Acknowledgements

The author and publisher would like to thank the following people and organisations for permission to use copyright materials in this book. It is important to acknowledge the museums and heritage sites that have been visited and used while researching the book too. I am indebted to those people who have assisted with personal and family stories, photographs and the loan of books and information.

Thanks is due to Michael Callaghan at Stott Park Bobbin Mill for his help with the information about the mill and the loan of photographs; with permission of English Heritage; Liz Critchley of Fell Foot for information and photographs courtesy of National Trust and visits to Blackwell, Brantwood, The Ruskin Museum, Wray Castle, Dove Cottage, Rydal Mount and Rydal Hall.

Thanks to the loan of photographs from Harriet Baxter, Kris Jepson, Wilkinson/Cowan family archive and Margaret Thwaites. This collection included photographs the family had from their time at Brantwood as members of the household staff. I have used many pictures collected over the years and postcards by Tuck, Valentine, Real, Sankey, Atkinson and Abrahams. I have tried to ensure permission for copyright material has been sought. However, if I have inadvertently used any copyright material without permission or acknowledgement I will make the necessary correction at the first opportunity.